A Time
Like No Other

My Journey 1946 -1947

KEN RAND

ISBN 978-1-969865-50-3 (Paperback)
ISBN 978-1-969865-51-0 (Ebook)

Inquiries and Book Orders should be addressed to:
Leavitt Peak Press
17901 Pioneer Blvd Ste L #298,
Artesia, California 90701
Phone #: 2092191548

For my brother Johnny and in Memory of our Mom, Dad,
and our siblings, Frankie, Binnie, and Judy.

And to my wonderful wife and our two sons, Kevin and Chris.

BOOKS BY KEN RAND

- Time Cards and Paychecks, Janus Publishers
- Beginning Algebra text: Solving the Mystery, Ken Rand Publishing
- Handy Math series: Focus on Sports/w Jan Fair, Creative Publications
- Handy Math series: Focus on Travel/w Jan Fair, Creative Publications
- Handy Math series: Focus on Purchasing/w Jan Fair, Creative Publications
- Point-Counterpoint: Creative Publications
- Habits of the Mind: contributing author Stylus Publications
- After Words (word game book), Ken Rand Publishing
* Second Chances, From Surviving through Thriving, Thyme Press
- One Student at a Time: A Teacher's Journey, Leavitt Peak Press
- One Teacher at a Time: Teach – Inspire – Change, Leavitt Peak Press

GAMES AND PUZZLES BY KEN RAND

- Dominque, Great Games • Dotto, Tega-Rand
- Shanghi Rummy, Brio International
- In the Chips New York, Tega-Rand
- Runners World Marathon, Tega-Rand
- Closure: Ken Rand Publishing
- Random (word games), Ken Rand Publishing
- Puzzles; Gifts of Chocolate, Tega-Rand • Puzzle; Poker Chips, Tega-Rand

FRONT COVER

- Designed by Mari Martin, Postal Graphic, Hollister, CA
- Photo (953): Sitting on bench (left to right): Cousin Debbie, Twin Cousins, Kay and Joanie, my sister Judy. Standing behind (left to right): Me (with the world's smallest tongue, Frankie, and Binnie

ENDORSEMENTS

1. Ken Rand's memoir *A Time Like No Other* is a delight on so many levels. It's his own coming-of-age story, full of humor, teenage angst, celebrity encounters, and brushes with danger; it sets the stage for the remarkable teaching career he chronicled in *One Student at a Time: A Teacher's Journey*; and it's a thumbnail history of American culture in the 1950s and 1960s. Throughout, Ken offers up a steady stream of personal stories, often hilarious, sometimes poignant, that will move and entertain you. Highly recommended! ....**Professor Jim Riley**

2. He did it again. First, he wins first place at the Los Angeles book festival for his memoir, "One Student at a Time," then he follows it up with a book that has become a standard for the education industry, "One Teacher at a Time", and now his new memoir "A Time Like No Other", which is sure to surpass them both. His story telling is a gift, one that I have not seen surpassed by any other author. I enjoyed every minute of his book, especially his candor and ability to weave in his personal stories with the "Breaking News" of the day. This book is as 'Timeless" as the memories he shares. ....**Veronica Garcia**

3. Ken Rand's new book is a true treasure. His storytelling instantly transports you back to the 1950s—a time when the world, New York City, and America as a whole were so different. Through his words, you don't just read about history— you experience it. His stories paint vivid pictures of daily life, full of color, humor, and heart. At one moment, you'll find yourself laughing out loud, and at another, deeply moved by the people and experiences he brings to life... **Professor Johnny Perez**

4. What a roller coaster ride of a life. From absolute trauma to incredible success. We are lucky to have an author whose conversational style of writing brings us along with him on his incredible journey. I love his reference to music and movies that helped to define his era. Fantastic. A must read.......**Mia Alvarado**

5. Ken Rand delivers again. With humor, heart, and unforgettable storytelling, he transports readers back to life in the 1950s—a world without today's technology but rich with love, family, and adventure. Every page feels like a conversation with an old friend, filled with wit and jaw-dropping moments from his remarkable life. A captivating memoir you won't want to put down." -**Dr. Patricia Garcia**

6. I too was brought up in the 50s and 60s. Thank you. Thank you, Ken, for this incredible journey. You brought me back to my growing years during "A Time Like No Other". There is something for everyone. It is amazing how he was able to remind us of the past but yet cautioned us not to live in it. I loved it. Five stars. **....David Eary**

7. Ken, my friend. Thank you. I could not put this book down. Your life adventures were truly unique. Many of us suffered the trauma of being in a dysfunctional family and, like you, have survived and thrived. You have shown remarkable strength and resilience. I am actually proud to say I read your book......**Tim Wallace**

8. As you did in your other memoir, "One Student at a Time" who have managed to move your reader to feel a variety of emotions. It doesn't get any better than that. I was not born in this era, but your stories and history notes are compelling. This was the most painless history lesson I've ever had. BRAVO, Ken......**Josh Oropeza**

9. In his latest book, Ken Rand takes the reader on a magic carpet ride filled with nostalgia for a time gone by. It was, as the title says, "A Time Like No Other." A time that will never be repeated again. This book is masterfully written and will remind readers of some of their

own childhood memories. I highly recommend it for everyone…. **Dr. Ken Harris**

10. Yes….you make me want to "Shout". With joy. So many iconic songs, music and tv shows were created in this era. Thank you for this incredible ride. I loved every bump and turn. Your stories about the negative events in your life bring hope to those you have had similar experiences. You made the right 'Choice'….**Rosa Bravo**

11. What a storyteller. Ken's new memoir, "A Time Like No Other" brought me down memory lane. His ability to weave his personal experiences with a touch of history is masterful. I highly recommend this book to everyone regardless of the year you were born….**Dirk Etienne.**

12. Ken has found a way to bring us down memory lane allowing us to keep our eyes open to the future. There are times when I cried and times when I could not stop laughing, (his Dumbo ears, etc.). You will thoroughly enjoy this memoir…..**Agnes C. Laurel**

13. I simply love your conversational style. It makes me feel that I am sitting across from you as you masterfully tell your stories. I love that you were able to take us with you on your journey during the 50s and 60s. So much happened in this era to change and influence our country and perhaps the world. You chose an amazing title for your memoir, it was for sure, "A Time Like No Other." Kudos to you…… **Professor Hetty Yelland**

14. Each generation has its contributions to society. Each brings its own unique changes and challenges. In this memoir, Ken has helped us appreciate the contributions of the 50s and 60s, a perspective I have not read before. Ken, you should have been a history teacher! I know I would have had a lot of fun learning from you!. Congratulations on a wonderful memoir…**Molly Orsetti**

15. I applaud your candor and bravery in telling us not only about the good times in your life but also about the bad times. I am sure that this was not easy to do. I sense that you did so because you have a message. I message of hope, which I thank you for. Thanks for making me laugh and cry. ... **Mike Willey**

16. Ken has a rare gift: the ability to connect with his readers in a way that feels personal and lasting. This book is not just a collection of memories, but an invitation to reflect, feel, and remember. A true gift of storytelling that will stay with you long after the last page... **Linda Reger**

17. Yes. I actually took your advice and got up, went to YouTube, and danced. And surprisingly my old legs still work, but you made it easy. I love how candid you are in relating to your personal experiences. I found this to be refreshing and honest. Thank you for making the events of the 50s and 60s enjoyable and meaningful and at the same time you found a way to intertwine your life's experiences. Well Done. ...**Linda Sachs**

18. He is not a famous actor, singer, or entertainer, but he has already written an award-winning bestseller and now, he has probably done it again. His ability to bring the reader to imagine that they are actually with him as he tells his tales is remarkable and fulfilling. To be honest, some of his stories do not seem possible. However, his candor sways the read to believe every word he has written. This book would make a great movie...**Doug Gonzales**

19. I enjoyed this book from start to finish. This book runs the gamut of emotions from laughing out loud to wiping the tears from your eyes. What a godsend. Thank you for sharing, and for reminding me how good it was when we were brought up. I can't wait for the movie to come out....**Judi Hersh**

20. Very moving and candid stories. I really believe that it would make for a great movie. I know this is a diamond. I can't wait to see

it on the bestsellers list everywhere. I love your conversational style of writing that brings me with you along the ride. You make your stories come to life. WOW. 5 Stars!....**John Moon**

21. Your ability to make fun of yourself is almost as priceless as your candor during the difficult times in your life. You have a special gift that allows the reader to feel your joy and pain. The '50s and '60s were special times for me. Thank you for sharing your memories. ....**Kacey Petre**

ABOUT THE AUTHOR

Ken Rand is an award-winning college math professor who retired in 2015 after 47 incredible years of teaching. Soon after retirement Ken became a presenter and guest speaker at numerous statewide and national educational conferences.

While working for Creative Publications (1977), Ken wrote and edited a variety of real-world activity books and some strategy games (*Dominque, and Shanghai Rummy*), which have been sold in stores such as Macy's, J.C. Penney and throughout Canada and Europe. He has also self-published his book of seven unique word games titled, "*After Words*" (1978, which also includes the original WORDLE).

Known for his classroom story-telling technique Ken has found a way to bring those classic experiences to life in his bestselling and award-winning memoir, "One Student at a Time". After reading Ken's book you will begin to realize that Ken has dedicated his life to making a difference in the lives of his students. His new memoir, "A Time Like No Other: My Journey 1946 – 1967," has even better reviews then his previous books.

To find out more about Ken, including the games he created, the books he has written and his speaking topics, please go to his website: **KenRand.net On this website you can find some great 'Bonus Chapters' for "A Time Like No Other."**

ACKNOWLEDGMENTS

There are so many people who have helped me along the way, and I will do my best to thank each one of you.

I am not a big fan of social media, but it was through these platforms that I was able to reconnect with some of my relatives and high school friends, who helped to bring back memories of events we enjoyed together. These friends include my best high school buddy Creighton Rayburn (Smoock, Smoock), (this is a private joke), Steve Einhorn, and two of my best high school friends, Shelly Flanders, Reggie Carlyle and Carolyn Ramin. I would also like to thank my three teaching colleagues and friends, Johnny Perez, Dr. Patricia Garcia, and Jim Riley. Their unconditional support and feedback made me a better writer.

In particular, I would like to acknowledge Jim Riley. As good as he was as a teacher, he may be an even better editor. What that means is that if you find any errors, we can blame them on him. Just kidding, any errors that you may find are solely on me. Jim spent countless hours going over and over my manuscript, and then he spent even more of his retirement time sharing his suggestions with me. His ability to fact-check my dates and events added accuracy to my stories. My two sisters-in-law, Linda and Linda Rand, were also there for me in the early stages of my book and provided invaluable suggestions to make my writing more organized and structured. I also would like to thank Marcy Tolkoff and Paul Thomas for their helpful suggestions.

I also want to thank my wife for her patience and support. It wasn't unusual for her to peek into my office and say, "You're so quiet. Are you all right?" or "Do you need anything?" She is a godsend. My two sons, Kevin and Chris, have always been supportive of my writing projects and are extremely helpful with their suggestions.

Kevin was there for me in the early beginning of this book and introduced me to some creative online editorial programs. His unconditional support and his knowledgeable suggestions are priceless. Lastly, I would like to thank my brother Johnny who proofread the sensitive and personal stories about himself and our mom and dad. His approval and encouragement to include these facts allowed more authenticity to my book.

CONTENTS

Part I: 1946 – 1951

Here are some stories from my early years. In these chapters, you will read about some early trauma, and you will also meet my family. Get ready for a trip down memory lane, filled with the nostalgia of the movies, music, and television shows during this era. At the end of this part, I have high-lighted some key historical events as well as some interesting facts about the current cost of living.

Part II: 1951 – 1955

In Part II, our family moves to Forest Hills in Queens, New York. An insurance check from the "Fire" allows us to upgrade our living standards. Of course, there is some more trauma, but there are also many great family adventures to read about. Again, at the end of Part II, you will see a list of important events and also how the cost of living might have changed.

Part III: 1955 – 1958

In Part III, we move again. Yes, another upgrade. It is a new place and a new time in history. So many great stories, especially the one when I get too mischievous for my own good. Our summer vacations in upstate New York became a meaningful part of my life.

Part IV: 1958 - 1963
In Part IV, we moved from New York City to a nearby suburb. Only 30 miles from NY, our new home seems like it is light years away filled with small town experiences, fresh air, and tree-lined streets. The peanut butter story, as well as "We want Rand", may have you on the floor laughing. Some of you may remember the Cuban Missile Crisis when, as a young teenager, I recall that the world as we know it may be over by 10:06 the next morning. I am older now, and the summers become even more memorable. There so many "do not miss" stories for you to read, and Rock 'n' Roll is at its peak. Get ready to dance.

Part V: Off to College

I should be excited, but I am very apprehensive. I am just 17 years old, and I am immature and lazy. Not a great combination for success on the college level. But these faults lead to some incredible stories revealing my true character and my big appetite. I graduated (I don't know how) in 1967. The world is changing and you will read about those changes through my stories, and in the "Breaking News".

INTRODUCTION

Why I Wrote This Book

Music, perhaps, more than any other medium, has the ability to transport us back to a specific time and place in our life.

For example...It's Saturday morning. May 25th, 2019. I was not looking forward to the three-hour bus ride from Santa Clara, California, to the Cache Creek Indian Casino. The bus was leaving at 8:00 AM, which meant that I would have to wake up around 6:00 AM. I hate waking up early, especially on weekends. My wife Vita is accustomed to waking up at this hour, and she quickly napped minutes after our trip started. It's not fair.

My intended nap on the bus was soon interrupted.

Throughout the entire trip, the bus radio was playing old songs from the 50s and 60s. These were my growing years. This, of course, was not the first time I would reminisce while listening to these songs, but I guess now that I am getting older, they seem to have more meaning to me. One of those songs, on the radio, "Pretty Woman", by Roy Orbison, brought me directly back to a Saturday night party when I was in high school. Another song, "In the Still of the Night," by the Five Satins, reminded me of the many nights my high school friends and I would sing under lamp post in front of our school.

Do Wop, Do Be Do, Do Wop, Do Be Do
Oh in the still of the night
I held you

Held you tight
'Cause I love love you so
Promise I'll never
Let you go
In the still of the night

Each song on the bus radio provided its own unique memory of growing up during a particular time in my life. Some of my memories are vague but most of them are very vivid. Listening to these songs was quite moving, and the nostalgia was overwhelming. I often thought that it was a shame that my sons don't know much about my past.

I am a storyteller, so most people I know (my friends, family, students, colleagues, and neighbors), have heard or read the stories about my teaching career and my roller coaster ride of experiences. But these are easy to share. Let's just say that my friends and family and those of you who are about to read this book are in for a surprise. There are stories in the book that I have only shared with my parents. Some of them will make you laugh, and some may bring you to tears.

The time in which I was brought up was a unique time The world was rapidly changing, but we still had rotary phones in our homes, and there were phone booths on street corners. Here's a short side story illustrating how different life was: I am now retired from teaching for 10 years. By the way, we were often told that retirement was supposed to be the 'golden years.' It's not true. They should have called it the 'wonder years.' At my age, I wonder where my keys are, I wonder where my phone is, and I wonder when and where I will have my next body ache.

Anyway, I need to see the doctor about a possible tear in my rotator cuff. In our current time in history, it may take weeks and sometimes months to get a doctor's appointment. When I was 13 years old, I recall coming down with the flu. My mom called our family doctor, Dr. Juliett, who took the time to do a house call during a winter snowstorm to come and see me. After examining me, he left with the usual doctor's refrain, "Give him two aspirins and call me in the morning. And chicken soup seems to help." This is a perfect example of one of the reasons why I am writing this book. It is now 2025. Can you even begin to imagine a doctor making a house call?

A Time of Innocence

Life was so simple then. Historians have labeled the '50s and '60s as a "time of innocence", and many feel it was the greatest generation. Those of us born in that era were also called the post-World War II "baby boomers." Up until that time, us baby boomers were the largest generation in US history, that was until the millennials took over the number one spot. I know that each generation, since then, may want to lay claim to being the best ever and that theirs was 'a time like no other'. But they would have a strong argument from me.

In the early 50s we witnessed the birth of television (in black and white). And it was live TV, where the unpredictable could—and would—happen, and laughter on a comedy series was genuine, and not scripted. TV and radio were the only technologies that existed at this time, and TV was a new source of entertainment and news. It is my guess that the word technology was never in anyone's vocabulary.

We did not have computers, cell phones, or calculators. Instead of using a calculator, we used an instrument called a slide rule for doing calculations. And the acronym SUV did not exist. People drove station wagons, and some families had a "Woody" wagon.

A "Woody" wagon (1946)

We felt safe, and it wasn't unusual for families to leave their cars and front doors unlocked. Think about this for a second. I don't know anyone living today who would purposely leave their car or home unlocked for any length of time.

It was also a time when rock and roll permeated the radio airways, and you could even understand the words of a song. Elvis was the King of Rock and Roll, and he helped redefine and perhaps can be credited with the cultural revolution that was soon to follow. And there were so many iconic groundbreakers: Frank Sinatra, Jerry Lewis and Dean Martin, Jackie Robinson, Willie Mays, Mickey Mantle, Rock Hudson, Marlon Brando, Marilyn Monroe, James Dean, Brigitte Bardot, Hugh Hefner, Rosa Parks, Dr. Jonas Salk, and many more.

Drugs were not the epidemic they are today. The only epidemic was polio, but the preventative vaccine was soon to follow. I'm not a big fan of 'living' in the past, but I am a big fan of the 'past.' Confusing? Let me explain. Living in the past prevents us from having an unimaginable future. However, embracing our heritage, and remembering the good things about the past puts 'today' into a different perspective.

Today's generation will likely struggle to understand what it was like when people communicated via talking on the phone, sending letters, or face-to-face conversations, rather than texting or emailing. If you go to a restaurant today and look around, you will notice that at least half of the people are on their cell phones. I don't know what they are doing, but I know what they are not doing.

When I was growing up, we also had a more robust sense of commitment to 'family,'. We had frequent Sunday night dinners together, and this was the norm rather than the exception. Things were so different then. The milk tasted different, and even water (*bottled water? What's that?*), and meat tasted different. The air was cleaner and even smelled better, much better. Oh, how I miss those tastes, and smells. It is difficult to describe how different they were, except to say that the food and air tasted and smelled fresher.

It was also a time when the women's rights and civil rights movement gained momentum. As I mentioned earlier, the world was slowly beginning to change in terms of economics, culture, and technology.

I have two goals in writing this book. One is to share my personal life journey and memories with you, and the other is to provide you with a picture of what was happening in the world, especially in this country, during the '50s and '60s. It is not my goal to pass judgement on the time in which I lived. I will leave that to the historians and sociologists.

My view of the world was very narrow. I was born into a white middle-class family in New York City. If I was born under different circumstances or if my skin color had been black or brown, or if I had been Asian or a woman, then my stories and experiences would have been very different. I do not know the answer to the question of what would be different, but I think it is important to ask it.

You will soon draw your own conclusions about whether the time in which we baby boomers were brought up was "A Time Like No Other." If you were born in the 50s and 60s, I know you will cherish this journey and my personal stories. If you weren't born in this era, then sit back, relax, read, and enjoy what you've missed.

Put on your seat belts and enjoy the ride.

Part I: 1946 – 1951

CHAPTER ONE

"The FIRE"

"Fiirrre...Fiirrre". That's me trying to tell a phone operator that our house was on fire.

My world, as I knew it, would soon change forever. The story that I am about to share is as vivid as if it happened yesterday. Sometimes it's a reckless decision that sets forth a chain of events that can alter one's history. One minute, life is normal, and the next minute can lead to chaos. It all happened so quickly. I was five years old when the impulse to play with a box of matches became the focus of my mischievous behavior. I was in my parents' bedroom, and the forbidden, but tempting box of matches, was on a table next to my parents' bed.

What happened next would help to define my fragile psyche, and its emotional impact would last for decades. While fiddling with one of the matches, it accidentally lit up. Within seconds, the entire matchbox that I was still holding burst into flames.

To keep myself from getting burned, I instinctively threw the matchbox, and it unfortunately landed in my parents' open clothing closet. Immediately, the entire closet burst into flames, including my mom's recent anniversary gift and prized possession, a mink stole; I panicked. I'm five years old. I didn't know what to do. I knew that I needed to get help. I quickly ran out of the room, closed the door, and rushed towards the front door, which led to the steps and the street.

I couldn't speak; words were incapable of coming out of my mouth. There was no time, and I had to get help. My mom was sitting on the living room sofa, and she shouted, "Where are you going?" No time for me to answer. When she saw me run almost literally through the front door, she said, "At least bring your coat; it's freezing outside."

There was no time to get my coat! I ran down the fourteen steps to the street, turned right, and ran about 100 feet to the nearby candy store, knowing that it had an indoor phone booth. When I reached the store, I headed right for the phone booth and kept dialing the rotary dial, "0" for the operator. After what seemed to be forever, she finally answered. Bad news. I still couldn't speak. No matter how hard I tried, I could not get the words that were raging in my brain, out of my mouth. Our apartment was about six stores further down directly above the laundromat.

The Candy (Drug) store on the corner of Cypress Avenue

Finally, I shouted "FIIRRE… FIIRRE", at which point the store owner knew something was wrong and started talking to the operator. The next thing I remember was standing in front of our apartment with the rest of my family. The fire trucks were parked in front of the laundry store where we had our upstairs apartment, and the firefighters were spraying water on the flames that were coming from our home.

My family members were all wearing their winter coats. It, it was one of those frigid January days in New York City. But I did not feel the cold; I was just happy that everyone was alive. Our apartment was totally destroyed. Almost nothing inside was saved. The cause of the fire was not yet determined, and no one knew it was my fault. In a few weeks, the fire department falsely blamed the fire on a faulty electrical switch. The significance of which will alter our future.

I did not confess my guilt (to anyone) until about 35 years later, when I had a nostalgic conversation with my dad about the good old days. At first, he did not believe me, but I was able to convince him by going into the details of the events. There wasn't much for him to say. He was just shocked that I never told him before.

You may be wondering 'why' I didn't tell anyone that I started the fire. Well, I think 'why?' may be the wrong question to ask. The better question could be, "Are you now okay?" The answer is 'Yes'. However, it is difficult to put into words the overwhelming feeling of shame and guilt that I subconsciously must have carried with me for the next thirty-five years. I was just five years old, and I just destroyed our home and every possession we owned.

While relaying the above story, I slowly began to remember the layout of our apartment. Living quarters were tight for a family of six. We had only two small bedrooms, so all four of us kids slept in one room. The largest room was the living room, which was only 12' by 12', and there was only one bathroom for the six of us. Using the toilet became an exercise in patience. There were times when all six of us were lining up to use the toilet.

I just remembered a joke from a comedian who performed at the hotel where my dad was the band leader. He was talking about the times in which he was brought up, "When I was young, we had eight of us in our family. Waiting on a line to use the bathroom was sometimes painful. Now I am very successful. Now I have a four-bedroom house in Beverly Hills, and we have six bathrooms. The problem is...now I can't go"!

POST-FIRE

Without a place to live, our family had to split up and live with different relatives. We were fortunate, however, to have family close by. My two older brothers, (Frankie and Binnie) and I went to live with our mom's sister, Aunt Marie. My younger sister (Judy), lived with my mom's brother, Uncle Bo.

Aunt Marie's apartment building

Aunt Marie's apartment was on the sixth floor, and there was no elevator. Living with Aunt Marie and her family was a unique experience. Aunt Marie always seemed to be cranky. "Don't touch this. Don't touch that". I am sure that my brothers and I were an intrusion on her lifestyle, but she was that way even after we moved out. I always felt that I was walking on eggshells.

4

It wasn't all bad. We lucked out when Aunt Marie bought a new Admiral TV console, which had all three components: a TV, a phonograph, and a radio all wrapped in one unit.

There was a classic television show in the '50s that we often watched together, called The Honeymooners. It starred the versatile Jackie Gleason, who was a comedian, orchestra conductor, composer, and professional pool player. I bring this up because, on this weekly comedy TV show, Ralph Kramden (Jackie Gleason) and his wife Alice frequently had conversations outside the kitchen window with their downstairs neighbors, Ed Norton and his wife.

These scenes were identical to the nightly conversations my Aunt Marie had when she talked through her open kitchen window with her nearby neighbors. The kitchen was very small, about 4' wide and 8' long, with barely enough room for a small table. It had that one window which opened to a view of other kitchen windows all looking over an alley way below.

My Cousin Gil (Aunt Marie's son) was 17 years old at the time, and he loved listening to opera, classical music, and jazz. Gil enjoyed having his cousins stay over and he introduced my brothers and I to the rhythmic sounds of jazz band leader, Benny Goodman, whose drummer, Gene Krupa, is said to be one of the best who ever lived. I remember Gil saying, "You've got to listen to this, you'll love it". Gil also enjoyed listening to the other great bands, such as. Duke Ellington, Count Basie, and the Dorsey Brothers.

While staying at Aunt Marie's apartment, Cousin Gil often played the Benny Goodman recording of "Sing, Sing, Sing," which had a hypnotic effect on me. It is hard not to move your body while listening to this instrumental song. This impromptu masterpiece by Goodman and his band became an all-time jazz classic and is featured in many movies.

Cousin Gil also introduced my brother Frankie to Tchaikovsky's 1812 Overture, and I think Frankie played that inspiring musical piece at our home every day for the next 10 years. If you have some time, go to YouTube and find the 1812 Overture. Close your eyes, and listen, you will soon see the marching soldiers while hearing the church bells ringing in the background. Between Gil's love of the classics and my dad's background in classical music, I had an early appreciation for music from all genres. Gil was also enamored with opera singer Enrique Caruso, (*O sole Mio)*, who some believe to be the greatest male tenor who ever lived.

Despite having to live with our cranky Aunt Marie, we adapted, but there were still too many days when I missed my parents. About four weeks later, I found out that my mom and dad were still sleeping and eating in the burnt-out apartment.

A few weeks went by before I finally returned to the apartment to visit my parents for the first time since the fire. I can recall the incredible shock I felt upon arrival. The water from the fire hoses destroyed everything that wasn't already blackened and charred by the fire, and it still had that unmistakable odor of fire and smoke. I don't have to try hard to recall that penetrating smell. Even the ceiling had huge holes in it.

As I walked up the 14 burnt and charred steps, I felt tears in my eyes when I reached the broken front door. I entered what used to be our apartment, and I could see my parents sitting in what was left of our kitchen. They were having lunch on a table that now had three legs. I was crying so much inside.

To think that I had done something to cause all this misery was overwhelming. Seeing the sadness on my face, my dad said, "Don't worry, Kenny. Everything will work out fine. It was just a freak accident, and no one was hurt. Within a few months, we will be moving to a new place."

My five-year-old brain was incapable of comprehending the word 'accident'. I am not a psychologist, but I do understand that guilt, shame, and abandonment do not always have to be conscious feelings. They are, unfortunately, held inside.

Being away from my parents for three months seemed like three years, especially to a scared and guilty five-year-old. My sense of abandonment (being separated from people I love), would turn out to be a recurring theme in my life. I am sure that over the next few years I might have had reason to recall this awful incident, but I know that over the next forty years, I hardly ever, on a conscious level, ever thought about the fire.

CHAPTER TWO

Early memories

- **My Family**

I have numerous early memories, but I should start at the beginning. I was born Kenneth John Temsky, on April 25, 1946, around 10 AM. It was a cold spring day (I just made up the weather part).

To the disappointment of my parents, Nathan and Margaret Temsky, I was their third consecutive son. After they married (1942), they made an agreement that any son born could be brought up Jewish, and if they had a daughter, she could be brought up Catholic. They also agreed and insisted that it would be our personal choice.

My oldest brother Frankie was born in 1943, my other brother Binnie, was two years older than me, and my sister, Judy, was one year younger than me. My brother 'Binnie' had an unusual nickname, which he received from our cousin Essie, who was unable to pronounce his given name of Jimmie (aka James) correctly. Her way of saying it was to pronounce it as Bimmie, which later shortened to Binnie. And it stuck with him his entire professional and personal life.

My dad met my mom when she knocked on his door asking for donations for a black family who did not have enough money to pay for their mother's funeral. My parents had a deep sense of compassion and empathy for those less fortunate than themselves. My parents were not rich—in fact, they were quite poor when they got married. Mom was a volunteer to help the homeless, and Dad was a struggling musician who paid the bills by selling insurance.

When they met, Dad was 23, and Mom was a young 17. They married two years later, somehow surviving some family turmoil that arose from their marriage. More about that later.

- **St. Mary's Park**

Another early memory includes playing with my older brothers and my sister in St. Mary's Park, which was about three city blocks from our apartment.

A recent photo of St. Mary's Park.

Nothing has changed since 1946. My siblings and I would frequently go to this nearby park and play cowboys and Indians (way before this became politically incorrect). We had toy guns, called cap guns, holsters, and cowboy hats, and we would hide from each other by scrambling around among what I thought were massive boulders, rocks, and trees.

"Bang… you're dead" was our usual conversation during our make-believe conflicts, and "Bang…I got you" was an often-repeated phrase even if it was not true. Or "Why am I always the one to get shot?" I recall visiting this park about twenty years later, only to be surprised by how small it was. A young kid's imagination is usually much larger than reality. I don't remember how often we played there but it seemed like we spent many hours there having too much fun. Most of the time, our only escort was Frankie who was about nine years old at the time. This is another example of how safe people felt in the early 50s.

There were always other games to invent, and one of them was hide and seek. In this game, one of us would close our eyes, count to a hundred, and then go looking for any one of our siblings. Over the years we must have hidden behind every tree and boulder in the entire park.

• P.S. 65

When I was five, I entered the first grade at the local elementary school, P.S. 65, which was within walking distance (two blocks) from our apartment. I know that I was the youngest student in the first grade, and it had nothing to do with my intellect. It was because my birthday, April 25th, came on one of the last days of April, allowing my parents to register me earlier for school.

From that day on, and throughout my entire educational career, I was always the youngest student in my grade, even in high school and college. The ramifications of being the youngest in my grade will be shared in later chapters.

P.S. 65 with a new makeover

I still remember my first-grade teacher's name, Mrs. Summers, but I'm not sure how old she was. I recall that she looked like she was 90 years old. She was sweet but also firm about discipline, especially during our lunch hour or recess break, which was often spent outdoors in the cemented schoolyard behind the school.

There is only one school memory of any significance that I can recall. One day, the school prepared a lunch meal that made my stomach very upset, and I threw up. The food was terrible. My mom soon came to the school and spoke to the principal about the awful taste of the cafeteria food. As a result, I was allowed to bring homemade lunch to school every day. This was my early introduction to peanut butter and jelly sandwiches. YAY.

- **Christmas in My Early Years**

My dad was Jewish, and his family was from Russia and Poland. My mom was Catholic, and her family was from Ireland and Spain.

It is somewhat unique and interesting that all my mom's sisters married Jewish men. Because of their different religious backgrounds, my mom and dad decided early on in their marriage to make some compromises as to how we would be brought up.

We celebrated Christmas every year, and my Jewish dad actively participated. I remember Dad always waiting until late on Christmas Eve to buy a tree at the lowest possible price, and I also remember attending Midnight Mass on Christmas Eve with my mom and siblings. Dad did not attend mass.

I do not recall, however, if we ever celebrated the Jewish holiday of Chanukkah. In the spring, we celebrated both Passover and Easter. I also don't recall celebrating the Jewish holidays of Yom Kippur and Rosh Hashanah, but I know that our dad ensured we were aware of them. It was not as complicated and confusing as I am making it sound.

Christmas in my early years and throughout my childhood had always been a special time at home. Every year, our relatives would come over to our apartment for Christmas dinner and the unwrapping of gifts. Throughout my growing years our apartment (or home) was the focal point of all of the holiday parties. Perhaps it was because we owned a piano and my dad would play the holiday songs and have the entire family sing those joyous sounds.

My mom cooked the best turkey and stuffing in the world, and we always had a large and beautifully decorated Christmas tree. I am beyond happy that my wife (Vita) learned my mom's stuffing recipe and can now duplicate both the flavor and memory of those meals.

One of the reasons Christmas was so special to me is that it also provided an opportunity to see my aunts and uncles, and cousins. My uncle Bo would predictably give all the kids two or three fresh and crisp one-dollar bills (depending on inflation). These one-dollar bills were so clean and fresh that I didn't want to spend or ruin them. I remember hiding them, usually between the pages of a book, to keep them fresh forever. Uncle Bo was a very happy person, always smiling and affectionate to us. He was short yet husky, with a large Irish face, and he could have passed for Santa himself if he were older and had a white beard. Below is a photo of us holding those brand-new one-dollar bills.

Uncle Bo is the first adult on the left, and my sister Judy is
next to him on the edge of the couch. That's me, with my plaid
shirt and elephant ears on the right front of the photo.

My aunt Marie always gave us underwear or socks. Yuk!
Unfortunately, (or fortunately), I do not have any photos of us hold-ing up our new underwear. Aunt Marie had a very unpleasant nick-name for me. She used to call me "Denny dimwit" (meaning, Kenny is stupid), and perhaps this is why I don't have many fond memories of her.

Even though we were not rich, my parents made sure that all of us received our favorite gift. The earliest Christmas I remember was when I was about four years old. My older brothers got a Lionel train set (I wish we had it now because they are worth a lot of money), and my sister and I got a "Coca-Cola" machine. I still remember opening the huge box, seeing the red and while Coca-Cola label, my eyes opened wide and instantly there was an unremovable smile across my face.

I also remember my older brother Frankie immediately opening the box of the train set and quickly building a train track around the Christmas tree. It was incredible fun. I felt like we were the richest kids on the block. The photo below is from Christmas morning 1950:

Left to right: Judy, me, Binnie, and Frankie, and
the Lionel train set is in front of us.

Throughout our childhood, we had to wait till Christmas morning to open our presents, and until I was much older, I never even heard of kids opening up presents the night before. My young (and now older) brain wondered how it could even be possible for presents to be under the tree on Christmas Eve, especially when Santa didn't arrive until midnight? Hmmm? It didn't make sense then and it doesn't make sense now. I guess when you are older it is no big deal. But when you are less than twelve, your belief in Santa should still be very real.

• **Holiday Movies**

I do not recall going to the movie theater until I was about six years old, however, television became a great source of current and past movies. I clearly remember watching numerous holiday movies on TV.

On Christmas Eve, our entire family would binge-watch the holiday classics. We would start on Christmas Eve with the movie, *It's a Wonderful Life*, starring Jimmy Stewart and Donna Reed. As midnight approached, we would watch the original version of *A Christmas Carol*, an adaptation of the book written by Charles Dickens. And then on Christmas Day, my siblings and I would enjoy watching *Babes in Toyland starring* the comedy team of Laurel and Hardy and then we would top it off by watching *A Miracle on 34th Street*.

Watching these movies while smelling my mom's turkey and stuffing in the oven is forever etched in my mind. For some reason unknown to me, the *Die-Hard* movies starring the charismatic Bruce Willis have become a holiday favorite, but to me, as entertaining as those *Die-Hard* movies are, they do not hold a candle compared to the older holiday classics.

Here's a modern holiday joke I just made up.

"Name your three favorite holiday movies"

Response: "Die Hard 1, hmmm........Die Hard 2, Die Hard 3."

That's kind of like answering this question...."Name the three best tennis players of all time, by answering..."Babe Ruth, Willie Mays, and Roberto Clemente."

• Mom' Family

My mom's family was very close. Not only is terms of their love for each other but they also happen to all live within walking distance of each other. This made family gatherings very large and enjoyable. I don't think there was a day that went by when at least one of her siblings was in touch with another. As I mentioned earlier, wherever we lived, our apartment (home) was always the gathering place for family parties or Sunday family dinners. Here is a photo of most of my mom's family (1951), taken a few months before the fire.

Front row: left to right. Me (and my big ears), Cousin Kenny, Cousin Essie, my brother Binnie, and then my sister Judy. In the back row, left to right. Patsy (my mom's best friend), my brother Frankie, Uncle Abe, Aunt Marie holding their daughter, Cousin Debbie, Aunt Cathy, Uncle Louis, and my beautiful mom.

For some reason, Aunt Junie and her twin girls, Kay and Joanie are not in the above picture. However, in the Family Album (after Part III) you will find some more family photos including my mom and her siblings.

- **Sunday Dinners**

My mom had a way of making those Sunday dinners very special. Each Sunday night, she would ask one of us, "What's your favorite?" and then she would cook our favorite meal as if she were a seasoned chef. On one Sunday, it could be roast beef, and the next one could be Hungarian Goulash, and the next would-be Spaghetti and meatballs, and there was always her fantastic meatloaf and Au Gratin potatoes. My favorite was Chicken Parmigiana with Penne pasta.

Most people will tell you that their mom was the best cook ever. However, when your friends and relatives ask your mom to cook her special spaghetti sauce (gravy), or turkey stuffing, then you know your mom's cooking is a notch above others.

- **Cousin Kenny**

Of all my cousins, the one that I was closest to was Cousin Kenny. Born three months after me, there was a family controversy over the fact that our moms chose to give both of us the same name. Who cares? Being the same age gave us an instant connection as playmates.

Some of my best memories from this time were going to his family's apartment for sleepovers. All of mom's siblings lived within blocks of each other, making it a short trip to go from one apartment to another. I remember the first time I slept over at Kenny's apartment. When I went to his bedroom, I saw something that I had only seen in magazines, which were bunk beds. To me, this was the coolest thing ever. When I was allowed to sleep over, we would alternate beds. One time he would sleep on the top bunk, and the next time he would let me sleep on the top. I use the word 'sleep', lightly because we were usually awake all night telling each other family stories.

Kenny's parents, Aunt Caty (mom's sister) and Uncle Louie, always treated me special, and they made me feel comfortable in their home. Kenny and I were not only close in age but also close as friends. About 20 years later, Cousin Kenny and I would teach together at the same Junior High School in the Bronx. I had already been there for three years and when he was hired, (with a little help from me), we were assigned to co-teach in a special program for emotionally disturbed boys.

Kenny and I continued to enjoy each other as friends for many years. We did lose touch when I moved to California (1976); however, we have since reunited. A few years ago, Kenny wrote a bestselling book titled, *Synchronicity: The Magic-The Meaning – The Mystery*. He then followed up this great book with an anthology, *Second Chances: From Surviving to Thriving*, which has become an Amazon bestseller. I am proud to say that I have a chapter in this book, titled *Making a Choice,* where I share my life-altering story. Cousin Ken is now a retired chiropractor and a leader in his field, as well as a gifted speaker who delivers motivational speeches nationwide.

- **Dad's Family**

You have met some members of my mom's family, so here is some background about my dad's family. A few months ago, this would have been a very brief story because I had never met or known anyone in Dad's family. That was, until recently.

My dad's family disowned him when he married out of his religion. Years ago, Dad shared with me that our mom, a devout Catholic, even took the ceremonial steps to be part of the Jewish faith, and they had both a Jewish and Catholic ceremony. But it was to no avail. My dad's mom would not forgive him. Unfortunately, Dad's mom influenced his dad and two sisters to also abandon him. I was told they even had a funeral for him.

Dad was always proud of his Jewish heritage and remained faithful until the day he died (April 23, 2015, at the age of 99 ½).

So, I never met any relatives on my dad's side of the family, until recently. A few months ago, I was playing golf with my friends at Ridgemark Golf Course (Hollister, CA.), where I now live, and the conversation turned to family. When I told my friends that I never met any of my grandparents they found it very difficult to believe. Both of my mom parents died before I was born.

Two days later, I received an email from my niece Candace, who lives in Long Island, NY. The gist of her email was that my dad's sister, Mary (whom none of us had ever met), had two daughters, Judi and Ellen. After their mom's recent death, Ellen, curious about her heritage and ancestors (especially my dad), did a DNA computer search and somehow found Candace (my niece) listed as a relative.

Within a few days, I now had the phone number of my long-lost cousin Judi, (Ellen's sister) who lives in California. I immediately called her, and we spoke for about an hour. We then decided to find a way to meet for lunch at an in-between location, which we did. We were so happy to finally connect that we must have looked and sounded like two little kids sharing an ice cream sundae.

Finding a lost relative, especially one as sweet and lovely as Cousin Judi and her husband Mark is thrilling.

(Left to right), Judi, me, my wife Vita, Judi's husband, Mark, and, of course, our pet Cavapoo, Ruby.

Not having grandparents from either side of my family left a void in my life. It wasn't always a conscious thought, but it would often creep in, especially when my friends told me that they were going to visit their grandparents or that their grandparents were coming over for the holidays. I remember instantly feeling envious and even jealous.

• Hit another one, Joe

Another one of my earliest memories is of my dad taking me to my first baseball game at Yankee Stadium. Dad, who was a work alcoholic, managed to find the time to take me to quite a few ball games. Strangely, I do not remember my brothers or sister coming with us. Dad knew I loved sports even when I was very young. Perhaps the constant throwing of my bottle out of the crib was the early practice of what would come later in my life.

Little did I know that this would be one of my last moments to spend with my dad before he headed off for the Korean War. This baseball game was on a Sunday in September of 1951. The stadium was packed with over 50,000 fans, and there were no empty seats.

I do not recall who the Yankees were playing, but there were a few events from that game that are still very vivid in my mind. The first one was the singing of the national anthem. Although I know I have listened to our country's anthem before, I had never heard it sung by 50,000-plus people, (most of them wearing fancy suits and dresses).

It sent chills up and down my spine. It was the first and last time (until 9/11) that I witnessed something so spectacular. I asked my dad if this had always been the case, and he was as puzzled as I was. Looking back, I wonder if this overwhelming display of patriotism was a result of our involvement in the Korean War.

Yankee Stadium during its heyday.

Our seats were in the upper deck, on the right side of home plate, behind first base. I remember looking out over the crowd at the stadium and marveling at how big it seemed to me. As a small kid at a huge baseball stadium, everything, especially the players, seemed so far away. However, the long distance between us and the baseball field did not diminish the sweet smell of the freshly cut grass. Having lived in the Bronx, my experiences with the scent of newly cut grass were minimal.

Joe DiMaggio was the hero of the Yankees and was loved by millions of New York and Italian baseball fans. He was one of the best players this game would ever see. This was to be his final season, and my guess, because of the size of the crowd, I might have been witnessing his last home game in Yankee Stadium.

Joe did not disappoint his fans. On his first trip to the plate, he hit a booming double, and then the next time up, he hit a tremendous home run. Each of these hits brought an immense roar and standing ovation from the packed stadium. When he came up for his third at-bat, I turned to my dad and asked him, in my five-year-old voice, "Can he do it again, Dad?" My dad said, "I don't know; why don't you ask him to do it?" I said, "What do you mean?" My dad said, "Go to the railing and tell him to do it again."

I quickly walked down to the overhand railing and shouted at the top of my voice, "Hey Joe, hit another ....". And before I could finish my sentence, he swung and hit another home run, his second of the game. I immediately went running up to my dad, shouting, "HE DID IT, HE DID IT," and my dad looked at me and smiled and said, "No, you' did it. He did it because you asked him to."

WOW! I began to think that I had this magical control over destiny. Being a prophet at the age of five felt pretty good. This whole experience was surreal. This was not just a baseball game. This was my very first baseball game to attend. The sights, sounds, smells, and of course, the taste of the stadium hog dog, were all new to me and are forever etched in my mind.

CHAPTER THREE

Television, Music, and Movies

- **Early Television**

My memories of watching TV during my early years are very vivid. Television was a new and primitive medium. In 1950, an RCA TV cost about $200. Although today, you can walk into Costco and get a nice 48" Television set for about $200.

A console TV combining a radio, phonograph, and TV altogether.

There were only two major networks at that time: Dumont and NBC (the National Broadcasting Company). ABC and CBS were not yet on the national scene. Imagine if someone from the future came back in time and said, "Someday you will have a choice between 500 TV channels." Only a crazy person would have believed them.

As young kids, our television time was limited, but I do recall watching the comedy/variety show, *You Bet Your Life*, starring Groucho Marx. Another popular show was the *I Love Lucy Show*, starring Lucille Ball and Desi Arnaz. Recently, the *I Love Lucy* show was recently voted as one of the top three all-time TV sitcoms.

My favorite TV show was the *Abbott & Costello show*. This comedy team rose to fame while entertaining American troops during World War II. They were radio, film, and TV stars and soon became the highest-paid entertainers in the world. Their routine of "Who's on first", is one of the greatest comedy skits of all time.

Bud Abbott on the right and Lou Costello on the left.

The first televised heavyweight championship fight, in 1946, between Joe Louis and Billy Conn, reportedly drew a TV audience of 141,000 people. However, here is an extraordinary statistic. My research shows that only about 8,000 people owned TV sets in 1946. My math tells me it is impossible for over 140,000 people to watch it on TV, unless each household had 17 guests invited over to watch that fight. Joe Louis knocked out Conn in the 8th round.

- **Music**

Music in the early '50s was uniquely different than the music of today. And it was also quite different than the music of the late '50s. The radio stations were dominated by male and female 'crooners' whose smooth voices and melodies could instantly drop your blood pressure by ten points.

I remember listening to the sounds of Perry Como, who had two number-one hits. Other greats of this era were Bing Crosby, Ella Fitzgerald, Nat King Cole, Dinah Shore (my mom's favorite), the Ink Spots, the Andrews Sisters, and Frank Sinatra.

Most people who weren't born in this era have no idea about Sinatra's popularity. He was the best of the best when it came to singing and was an earlier version of Elvis in terms of crowd appeal. He did not shake his hips, but I was told by my mom, that he had these penetrating blue eyes that captivated his female admirers. I have seen videos of Sinatra singing at sold-out concerts where women would be in a screaming frenzy throughout his entire performance. Below are some lyrics to one of his most famous songs.

Fly me to the moon
Let me play among the stars
And let me see what spring is like
On a-Jupiter and Mars
In other words, hold my hand
In other words, baby, kiss me

My dad, when driving us around, would often turn on the radio to listen to his kind of music, which was either classical or jazz. I remember listening to the jazz singer Cab Calloway, who rose to stardom in the 1940s and was still going strong into the 1950s. His most famous song was *Minnie the Moocher*. Is anyone out there old enough to remember the lyrics shown below to another song made famous by Cab Calloway?

Hi-de hi-de hi-de-hi (Hi-de hi-de hi-de-hi)
Hey-de hey-de hey-de hey (Hey-de hey-de hey-de hey)
He-de he-de he-de he (He-de he-de he-de he)
Hi-de hi-de hi-de-hi (Hi-de hi-de hi-de-hi)

All of us in the car would repeat his words while laughing and smiling throughout the entire trip. I have seen Cab Calloway perform in person, and it was thrilling to hear him inspire his entire audience to hypnotically repeat the above nonsensical words (shown in parentheses) in unison. I felt like I was witnessing a Church revival.

- **Movies**

The only movie I remember watching in the movie theater was *The Bridge on the River Kwai*, starring Alec Guiness. I can clearly recall my brothers and I marching like soldiers and trying to whistle the theme song all the way home from the movie theater.

Some of the box office hits in this era were *Notorious* directed by Alfred Hitchcock, *The Best Years of Our Lives*, *The Treasure of Sierra Madre*, *Black Narcissus*, *All the King's Men*, *All About Eve*, and *Vertigo*, (another Hitchcock thriller). The movie, *Singing in the Rain*, made a star out of dancing sensation Gene Kelly. And as great as Gene Kelly was, the honor of being the best American dancer went to movie star Fred Astaire.

The most popular actors of this time were Humphrey Bogart, Cary Grant, Ingrid Bergman, Gary Cooper, James Stewart and Bette Davis. John Wayne, and Katherine Hepburn. Because of the quality of movie makers and actors during this era, many historians call this the "Golden Age of Hollywood." Years later I was able to watch all of these classic movies.

In June of 1951, after my parents received a sizeable check from the insurance company for the fire damage, we upgraded our living quarters to a new apartment in Forest Hills, Queens.

Shortly after we moved to Forest Hills, my dad went to Korea for two years and there were many times when I thought he would never come home. His absence created a sense of loss that will change our lives.

BREAKING NEWS 1946 - 1951

Did you know that in….

- **1946** Harry Truman was President of the United States.
- The U.S. population was 141 million/life expectancy was 63 years.
- The United Nations had its first session.
- This year marked the official beginning of the "baby boom".
- **1947** A mysterious object crashes in Area 51.
- Chuck Yeager breaks the sound barrier.
- **1948** The creation of the state of Israeli.
- Racial segregation in ended in the U.S. military.
- Indian Prime Minister Ghandi is assassinated.
- **1949** The Soviets successfully test their first nuclear bomb.
- NATO is established.
- The Arab-Isreal war is ended.
- **1950** North Korea invades South Korea marking the start of Korean War.
- **1951** First color TV broadcast.
- 1he 22nd amendment/ limiting presidency to two terms.
- The U.S. population is 155 million.
- Our average life expectancy is now 68 years.

Famous people born:

- **1946** Sylvester Stallone, Cher, Dolly Parton, Bill Clinton, Donald Trump, and Andre the Giant.
- **1947** Kareem Abdul-Jabbar, Hillary Clinton, Arnold Schwarzenegger, David Bowie,
- **1948** Billy Crystal, Samuel Jackson, James Taylor, Al Gore.
- **1949**, Lionel Richie, George Foreman, Richard Gere, Meryl Streep
- **1950**, Stevie Wonder, Marilyn Monroe. Jay Leno.
- **1951**, Robin Williams, Phil Collins, Dale Earnhardt,

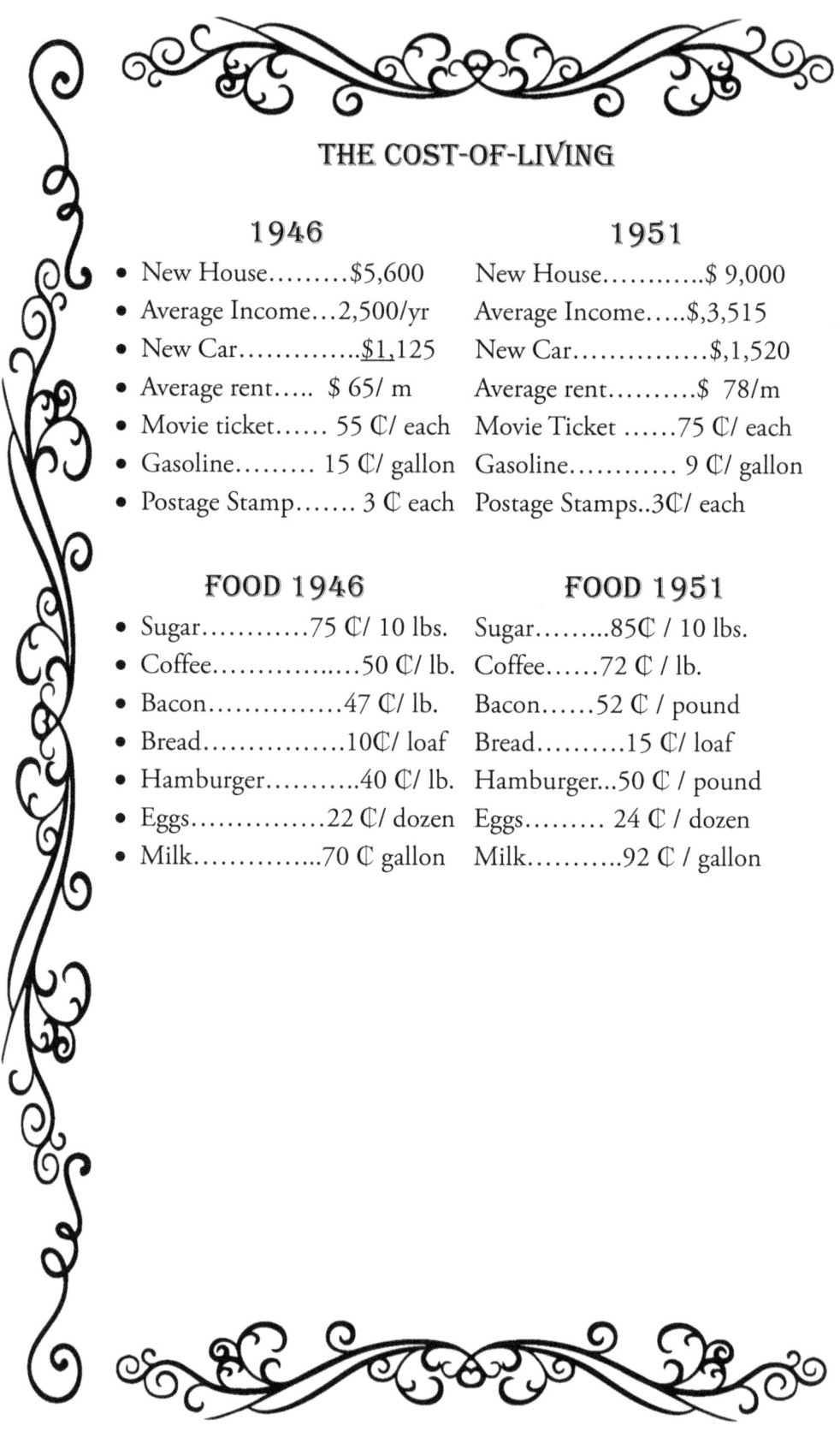

THE COST-OF-LIVING

1946

- New House………$5,600
- Average Income…2,500/yr
- New Car…………..$1,125
- Average rent….. $ 65/ m
- Movie ticket…… 55 ₵/ each
- Gasoline……… 15 ₵/ gallon
- Postage Stamp……. 3 ₵ each

1951

- New House…………..$ 9,000
- Average Income…..$,3,515
- New Car……………$,1,520
- Average rent………..$ 78/m
- Movie Ticket ……75 ₵/ each
- Gasoline………… 9 ₵/ gallon
- Postage Stamps..3₵/ each

FOOD 1946

- Sugar…………75 ₵/ 10 lbs.
- Coffee……………..50 ₵/ lb.
- Bacon……………47 ₵/ lb.
- Bread……………10₵/ loaf
- Hamburger………..40 ₵/ lb.
- Eggs……………22 ₵/ dozen
- Milk…………...70 ₵ gallon

FOOD 1951

- Sugar……...85₵ / 10 lbs.
- Coffee……72 ₵ / lb.
- Bacon……52 ₵ / pound
- Bread………..15 ₵/ loaf
- Hamburger...50 ₵ / pound
- Eggs……… 24 ₵ / dozen
- Milk………..92 ₵ / gallon

Part II: 1951 – 1955

CHAPTER FOUR

Forest Hills, Queens (108th St)

- **Our New Apartment**

During my childhood, our family moved three times. Though each move brought a sense of loss, it also gave the opportunity for new adventures. The loss was not only being further away from my mom's family and my cousins and friends, but there was a loss of comfort in the familiarity of one's surroundings. However, this loss is only temporary. Hopefully, with our new move, I can slowly begin to put the trauma caused by the fire behind me. However, as you will read later in this chapter, things do not always go as planned.

At that time of our move (July 1951), Forest Hills was experiencing rapid growth as it quickly became a middle-class mecca of New York City. It didn't take long for me to embrace our new environment. There were new friends, new sights, sounds, and smells to enjoy. Like the Disney song says, it was a "Whole New World." I recall feeling a deep sense of excitement and wonder.

Queens is one of the five boroughs that are in NYC; the other four are Manhattan, Brooklyn, Staten Island, and, of course, the Bronx. It is somewhat strange that the Bronx is one of the few places in the United States that can only be said using the word "the". Think about it. No one ever says, "The South Dakota."

All the apartment buildings on our block were built within the last two years. and were made of red brick, which was strikingly different from the gray (many shades of gray) buildings in the Bronx. Our new block had six of these apartment buildings. There were three on the left side and three on the right, all separated by a landscaped and groomed walkway with grass and bushes. Each apartment building had six stories, a basement, a laundry room, and storage rooms.

The streets were lined with beautiful trees, and there were some empty lots nearby that had boulders, hills, and trees inviting my brothers and me to play and explore. As a five-year-old, this new place that we now call home seemed as if we had moved to a different country, which is somewhat accurate because I am sure we brought our Bronx accents with us.

Our apartment was a corner unit on the first floor, facing 108th Street in the front and 63rd Avenue on the side. Both streets on the left and right of ours also had six identical apartment buildings, but the block directly across from 108th St and the block directly behind us were vacant, waiting for us to enjoy and explore.

My bed is next to the window directly to the left of the blue sign.
My brothers beds are next to the two windows above the tree.

The location of my window also provided another great memory for me, in that I would often open it late at night during the Fall and Winter, to breathe in the cold fresh air. Wow...I long for that smell again.

Although our new apartment was much larger than our previous one in the Bronx, my brothers and I still had to share one bedroom. However, this room was the best in the apartment because it had a great view with windows facing both the front and side streets. It was also right next to the living room and close to the bathroom.

• **The Aquacade**

A few blocks away from our apartment was a building called the Aquacade. This swimming and diving competition site was built for an earlier New York World's Fair (1939) and was one of only two buildings that remained from that event. The Aquacade remained open to the public as a swimming venue.

Every Thursday night in the summer, beginning at 9:00 PM, the Aquacade had a spectacular fireworks show, and guess whose bed had the best view? The problem was that I was the youngest and smallest of three brothers, and my two older siblings would usually jockey for the best position, which almost always blocked my view. Luckily, the fireworks exploded high in the bright and clear night sky, allowing me to share in their wonder. The show typically lasted around 20 minutes, and it became an event that we all eagerly anticipated every week.

About once a month, during the weekend, my mom would take us to the Aquacade to enjoy swimming and to learn how to dive. That soon stopped when mom became anxious about the rapidly growing Polio Epidemic. From 1950 to 1955, the United States was hit with an epidemic of the polio virus. During that period, over 52,000 Americans contracted this disease, and over 3000 kids under the age of five died from it. Many of those who lived were left paralyzed in one or both legs.

It was a contagious virus, and it primarily affected the young. This virus caused panic among parents, many of whom would no longer allow their children to go swimming, to the movies, or to any public event. The virus ended in 1955 when Dr. Jonas Salk created the polio vaccine, which was widely distributed to schools and family doctors. Unlike the COVID-19 vaccine, this cure was readily accepted by the American public. No one that we knew nor in my family ever contracted this virus.

- **Good Humor**

An enjoyable constant during this time (1950s) was the Good Humor ice cream truck. Who likes ice cream? Most of us do, especially me. In the 1950s and 60s, there was an ice cream franchise called Good Humor, which had a white truck that drove around the neighborhood and made daily visits to all of the apartment complexes. The Good Humor truck would stop at our block at least once a day during the Spring and Summer, and then it would proceed to the next block, and then the next.

A typical Good Humor truck was always surrounded by kids.

The ice cream truck would usually arrive at the same time each day, loudly ringing its bell to let kids know it was nearby. Like Pavlov's dog, we soon ran to the truck, wondering which ice cream product to buy. There was so much to choose from; maybe I'll try a different one each day? The ice cream truck had over 30 different choices.

A very popular choice was a chocolate sundae that was sealed in a small round container with a cardboard lid, and its bestseller was a 'creamsicle' made with orange sherbet and vanilla ice cream on a stick. My favorite was a chocolate crunch on a stick, which had vanilla ice cream covered with chocolate syrup and crushed peanuts. Yum…I would eat one now if it were within arm's reach. The fact that the truck arrived at the same time every day became a source of excitement for us kids (and adults, and dentists).

• **Dad Goes to Korea**

I am not exactly sure when my dad went to Korea, but I believe it must have been in 1951, and I recall that it was just a few short months after we moved from the Bronx. I am also unsure if he was drafted or volunteered for the service. I do, however, remember the empty feeling of knowing that I would not see my dad for a long time. Here is that story.

In 1951, the United States began sending its troops to help the fight against a communist regime in North Korea. The war ended in 1953, and the two years of our direct involvement would have a significant impact on my life.

Dad, a captain in the Army, was assigned to the USO entertainment troop, which traveled to different army camps in Korea, Japan, and the Philippines. My dad was a musician and played the piano, organ, and accordion (among many other instruments). Dad was gone for two long years, which seemed like a lifetime to me. Rarely seeing him for three months directly after the fire was bad enough. But, for a young 5-6-year-old, those two years that he was in Korea seemed like an eternity, and I honestly remember thinking, at times, because of the infrequent contact, that my dad may never come home. His letters to us were few and far between, and I remember one phone call from overseas when I was crying my eyes out, hearing his voice for the first time in about a year.

After that, I again dreaded that he might never come home. Suddenly, one day, to my incredible surprise and delight, he was home. Though Mom already knew he was on his way back from

Korea, she didn't tell us because she wanted to surprise us. Not only was he home, but he brought home duffel bags of overseas gifts and toys for all of us. I still remember some of those gifts. One was a beautiful silk Korean jacket, which had colorful stitching on the back, and the other was a realistic-looking toy Japanese samurai sword.

You can imagine that my dad's arrival home was sheer happiness for everyone. For someone who thought of the possibility that my dad was dead, this was a feeling of indescribable and unexplainable joy.

Those two years that Dad was away were also very challenging for my mom. Not only did she have to take care of four bratty kids, but she also had to start working to help pay the bills. Having limited contact with her own family, who still lived in the Bronx, along with her loneliness for dad, and her frustration in taking care of us, took its toll on her beautiful personality. At that time, I had no idea that my dad's time in Korea was the possible cause of her need to relieve her pain through alcohol.

Looking back, it is now understandable why she made this choice. For us kids, not only were we physically abandoned by dad, but we were also emotionally abandoned by our mom, who was contending with her own pain. My dad's physical absence, combined with my mom's emotional absence, had a profound effect on my own self-worth and identity. Though my siblings and I were very close, the inability to share our feelings became a recurring theme between us for the rest of our lives. People often overuse the phrase, "I have no regrets," but it is undeniable that our ability to overcome life's obstacles would have been a little easier if we had shared our feelings with each other.

Are kids of that age even capable of expressing these feelings? My fears of abandonment were probably a catalyst that led to this next incident in my life.

• Playing Hooky

It's 1952, and I am six years old, my dad is still in Korea, and I am in the second grade at Annadale Park Elementary School in Forest Hills. In the mornings, my siblings and I would walk the three short blocks to school. For reasons that I cannot remember (or maybe I have blocked them out) I didn't stay in school; I just sat on the steps at one of the school's outdoor side exits and stayed there all day until school was dismissed.

After school, I found my siblings, and we all walked home. I never told them that I had skipped school. I skipped school for five straight days until someone in the school office called my mom and asked her why I was absent. My mom was shocked because she saw me go to school and come home every day.

Mom was not mad at me; she just wanted to know why I didn't attend school. I could not tell her why, because I don't honestly remember, but my best guess is that it happened for several different reasons.

Perhaps it was because I felt 'stupid'. I might have had an inferiority complex, thinking I was not as bright as my classmates. Or, perhaps, my truancy was a way for me to act out because I missed my dad, who was in Korea at the time.

It is somewhat amazing that after seventy years, nothing about the structure of this school has changed.

In front of the blue doors is a small step and
this is where I was for five days.

• **More Trauma**

One of my Christmas gifts from mom and dad (1953) was a toy bow and arrow. However, one day, my excitement and glee turned into a tragic accident.

It was in January and I was playing with a friend outside our apartment building (there was snow left over from a recent storm). We were shooting the arrows against the outdoor walls of our apartment building and we were lucky to get the rubber tip to stick on the wall, and we would earn a point. Then we found some chalk and drew small targets on the wall, which added to our fun. We soon wanted to test the limits of my toy, and we tried to see how far the arrows would fly. Not satisfied, I then wanted to see how high it would go, and I took a practice shot (which initially had a rubber tip), go straight up into the air.

Yes...The worst possible thing happened. Somehow, the tip of the arrow fell off in flight, and the arrow came straight down and hit my friend directly in his right eye. What happened next is all very surreal and foggy. I remember the sounds of the ambulance and the parents of both of our families arguing, but that's about it.

My parents knew it was an accident and realized that I must have felt terribly guilty, and I remember them giving me a lot of comfort and support. But an 'accident', that I was a part of, became tragic for a family whose son lost his eye. The weeks following this incident are still foggy. I don't remember any further discussions, and I don't even know if my siblings knew about it. I do recall that my friend and I never played together again.

Here is quick story of another injury that was on a personal level. I was eight years old, and I was beginning to get interested in playing sports. Three blocks away from our apartment was Forest Hills High School, where my friends and I would practice baseball. One day, the entrance to the baseball field, which was protected by a 12-foot wire fence, was locked. We were determined to play, so we began to climb the wired fence despite its daunting height. When I reached the top, my hand got stuck in the exposed steel wires, which formed a "V" shape. OUCH!!

No matter how much I tried, I could not free my hand, which was penetrated by the wires. My only choice was to try to jump off the fence. I wonder if the top of that fence still has part of my hand. After a few stitches and two months later, my hand returned to normal, but seventy years later, the one inch 'V' shaped scar is still on my right hand. Time to move on.

- **The Future is Here**

In 1953, Chevrolet had just introduced the first American sports car, the Corvette. The base price of this fancy vehicle was $3,498. Don't worry if you missed out on getting one; you can buy a used one on eBay for only $186,000 or a brand-new 2025 Corvette for $ 70,000 to $178,000.

A 1953 Corvette Convertible

CHAPTER FIVE

Family Time

- **Piano Lessons**

When Dad came home from Korea, he bought a brand-new baby grand piano. The photo below shows my beautiful mom sitting at our new piano on Christmas Day, 1953.

My mom is just posing. She didn't even know how to play Chopsticks.

Shortly after my dad's return from Korea and with my mom's encouragement, dad found the time to give me and my siblings Saturday morning piano lessons. For one year, Dad gave piano lessons to all four of us, but he soon realized two things: one was that his four children did not possess his musical gift, and the other was that the time he spent with us was unproductive and could have been used to earn extra money on the weekends. Feeding and clothing the four of us can get expensive.

After that first year, I did manage to make a little progress, and Dad continued to give me those Saturday morning lessons for the next three years. My own talent was sadly somewhat limited. Dad was born with perfect pitch and could even tell you what 'key' you were talking in. My pitch was far from ideal.

I found the too many hours of practicing the piano to be boring. I wanted to play 'songs' that I heard in the movies or on the radio. My dad, however, wanted me to master the basic scales and the critical task of reading music. Both of which were too tedious for me. It's not that my dad gave up on me; it was more that I gave up on myself. Someone very famous said, "A man must know his own limitations," but then someone even smarter later said, "My only limitation is my own imagination." I love that quote.

Our Mom, however, didn't give up on any of us and had fantasies that her four kids would be stars in the entertainment industry. After our collective failure as pianists, Mom thought that there was a possibility that we might become a singing group. She even hired a singing coach for all of us. I'm not sure if it was possible to be any worse at singing than at playing the piano, but…we were also terrible at singing hitting sour note after sour note.

We were so bad that when we practiced our singing, Dad would ask us to stop because it was hurting his sensitive ear. To give you an example, when I sang in the shower, the shower would politely shut off because it didn't want to hear me sing either. Many years later, I taught myself how to play show songs or songs I heard on the radio, and this prompted Dad to hire a piano teacher for me, but this is a story for a later chapter.

• Dr. Death

This story is not about a great time; however, it was an annual family activity. Though we now lived in Queens, we still had our family dentist in the Bronx. His name was Dr. Roses (aka Dr. Death). Once a year, my dad would drive all of us to the Bronx to see the infamous Dr. Death. That first car ride to see him was emotionally scary, but the ensuing years brought with it a ride filled with fear, pain, and tears (even before we arrived there).

I recall the many occasions when a carload of my siblings and me would be crying during the entire trip. Dad would often have to bribe us with something special (like an ice cream Sundae) just to get us into the car (willingly?). Of course, the ice cream Sundae helped to explain why we had to go to the dentist in the first place.

To make it simple, Dr. Roses must have been a sadist. His sitting room was always full of about 10 to 12 people waiting for the upcoming pain, and he was in a one-man office. You need to understand that dentistry in the 50s was not very sophisticated, and technology was nonexistent. Even the "speed" drill had not yet been invented.

His office of pain, with its antique equipment, was located right next to the sitting room. These two rooms were separated by a curtain (not a door), and I believe he purposely left the curtain open so that the waiting patients would hear the screams of those he was treating.

For a group of four young kids, this was inhumane torture. His dental drills were slow (very slow), and he rarely used Novocain. Dr. Roses seemed to take pleasure in using as little Novocain as possible. I can still hear the sound of that slow drill and patients screaming in pain. Sitting in that waiting room, waiting for the upcoming pain was like a scene from a sadistic movie. Binnie, Judy, and I sat in constant fear with our knees shaking and tears rolling down our faces. Frankie, however, tried to be the brave one, and I don't remember him ever showing any fear.

There was a paradox to Dr. Death in that he would frequently give kids a gold-painted charm (for a bracelet?) after he killed them.

He had a large variety of these charms to choose from, so given enough time in your life (if you didn't die from the pain), you may be able to collect all of them.

I have a perfect example of the extent of his sadistic nature. When I was about ten years old, dad had to rush me from our summer vacation in the Catskills and drive three hours to the Bronx because I had a very painful toothache. It appears that one of my molars was trying to burst through my gums, and the pain was unbearable.

Well....that immediate pain was the least of my problems. Without any Novocain, Dr. Death took a medical tool with a small iron circle (about ¼ inch), then put it under a flame, and without any hesitation or pain killer, he burned the gum off the top of my tooth, allowing it to be exposed so the tooth could naturally grow.

I can still remember his infamous words, "This may hurt a bit." Are you kidding me? The word "hurt" does not even begin to describe that pain. Dr. Death did not have enough charms to make me feel better. My dad's loyalty to Dr. Roses was somewhat confusing. Perhaps the price was right, or maybe his acts of terror were an exchange for piano lessons. The next story may help explain our need to go to the dentist.

- **Urban Halloween**

Halloween night in an apartment complex is unlike Halloween anywhere else. Each Halloween, the four of us would attack all the apartments on our block with our supply of empty grocery bags, which we would eventually fill up with tons of candy. We had so much candy that sometimes we had to make a pit stop back home to empty the shopping bags, only to head out again in pursuit of sugar heaven.

Here's the simple math. Each of the six buildings on the block had six floors, and each floor had about 12 apartments. Multiply that by four kids. The math equation would look like this.

$$6 \times 12 \times 4 = \text{A lot of candy}$$

If you had the misfortune of living in a neighborhood with nothing but single-family homes, your mathematical options were much more limited than those of us who were brought up in an apartment building complex.

It was a time when some people asked you to do a trick to get a treat. And we were taught to say, "Thank you," after receiving our treats. I recall several occasions when we were all required to sing or dance; and sometimes, I would even play the piano to earn candy.

Some people would also give us money (coins such as pennies, nickels, and dimes) instead of candy. I remember one Halloween when the four of us netted about $81 in coins. Not bad. Eighty-one dollars can buy a lot of candy. BOO!

- **Daytime fun**

For our daily entertainment we participated in a variety of activities. In the 50s, there were no video games or computers, so we had to invent our own games and activities. Our favorite thing to do was to walk to a nearby empty lot that, even though it was void of apartment buildings, was not 'empty' to us. There were hills, trees, huge rocks, and countless hiding places.

The four of us spent hours playing hide and seek, cops and robbers, and anything else that came to our imagination. It was our opportunity to invent a world of fun and excitement. I remember also bringing some empty jam jars to start my bug collection, which always sent my mom into a minor rage of fear. Sometimes I would try to find the most enormous bug possible just to scare my mom even more.

Another game we played involved a homemade toy we called a "zip" gun. Let me explain. All the apartment buildings had huge cement porches or decks covered in a tar-like linoleum top. After a few years of wear and tear, the covering started to chip, allowing us to peel off small pieces.

These small pieces became the perfect ammunition for our wooden guns, which we made with a knife. Using a small nail, we would attach a rubber band to the back of the toy gun, then stretch the rubber band and release it, allowing the piece of tar to fly like a missile, traveling approximately 50 feet.

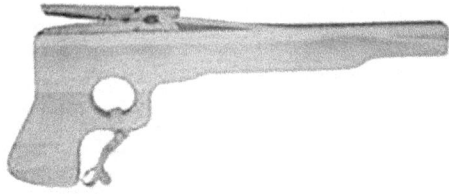

The photo above shows a typical zip gun.

Quite often, we would have wars between the kids on our apartment porch with those who lived across the way (about 30 feet away from each other). There was even a protective four-foot railing surrounding each porch, allowing us to duck away from the oncoming missiles of torn tar. Luckily, no one ever got hurt.

The photo below shows the combat zone,
directly in front of our apartment.

- **Winter**

Winter brought some special and different types of daytime fun, especially when it snowed. The facts are, contrary to popular belief, it rarely snows in New York City. It may be different in upstate New York, but NYC has a cold and dry climate in January and February.

Snowing during Christmas is even rarer. Sometimes we would have no snow at all for two months, and then there were times when it snowed for seven days in a row. It was very unpredictable. When it did show, it had the potential to be Winter Wonderland. I recall when I was six years old, we had a huge snowstorm.

The next day mom dressed me up in a snow suit. A word about snow suits. These suits could be the most uncomfortable clothing ever designed. Here I am, ready to go out in the snow, and my arms and legs are too stiff to bend. Throwing a snowball in this condition is impossible and even comic.

All I can do is stand still like a robot in a snowstorm. Even Mom laughed when I tried to move. As I started to walk, I was so stiff that I fell face down into about a foot of snow, and I was stuck. I'm trying to get up, but it's impossible. Luckily, my brother Frankie, after he stopped laughing, got me upright. There is a scene in the classic movie "A Christmas Story" where the young boy (Randy, "I can't put my arms down") gets dressed up in a typical snowsuit. Watch it. You will laugh for a long time. It's time for me to change my clothes and go back to warm pants and a heavy coat. Ah…let the snowball fight begin. Being in the city when it was snowing was magical. It's like a scene from a movie. What a treat.

These next few paragraphs have nothing to do with winter daytime fun. So, have you even been to New York in the Fall? I don't mean New York City, but I am referring to upstate New York? It is absolutely breathtaking. Other than Central Park, the city had few locations where there were lots of trees. However, upstate, even just 30 miles outside the city, the entire landscape is nothing but mountains with an abundance of trees.

When I was younger, the Fall season, with the changing colors of the leaves, would usually begin around the first week of October, and the further one would drive upstate, the more spectacular the scenery would get. Not only the colors, but the cooler air in October smelled so fresh. This is by far my favorite time of the year.

This photo is taken in upstate New York showing
the magnificent array of colors.

- **Ride em' Cowboy**

One of my fondest family memories as a young kid was going to the National Rodeo held at the original Madison Square Garden in NYC. Each year, My Uncle Abey would take me and my cousins (about 8 of us) to this exciting and sold-out event.

In the 1950s, there were two very popular cowboy actors, who were also singers, and both of them had hit records; Among Gene Autry's hits were "*Back in the Saddle Again, You Are My Sunshine* and *Tumbling Tumbleweeds.*" These songs were so popular that they are still sung at rodeos today.

It was Roy Rogers and his wife, Dale Evans, who hosted the annual event at the Garden. Their rodeo was a spectacle that had a mixture of riding skills and music. I clearly recall when they had the lights in the stadium turned off with just a spotlight on the two of them when they sang the songs, *"Happy Trails", "The Yellow Rose of Texas",* and *"Faith, Hope and Charity."*

What made it even more thrilling is that they asked the entire 15,000 people in attendance to stand up and sing along with them, and to my surprise, everyone knew all the words. It was quite memorable. Oh, I almost forgot Roy Rogers' beautiful horse named "Trigger", was a pretty good dancer and put on quite a show.

Another fun family event was attending the Ringling Brothers Barnum and Bailey Three-Ring Circus, also held at Madison Square Garden. This time it was my mom who was our constant chaperone. Clowns, acrobats, elephants, it was almost overwhelming. So much to absorb, so much to see. Another Wow!

- **Frankie**

My brother Frankie would attend these events with us, and he always made sure that his younger sister and I were safe. He held our hands as we crossed the street and always looked out for us when we were in school. That was the good side of Frankie. The downside was that, being the oldest, he was kind of a bully when it came time for us to watch TV.

He always took control of the TV set when the four of us were allowed to watch. If we wanted to watch TV, we were forced to watch his favorite shows, which were mostly horror movies or wrestling. Binnie did not always agree, and during TV time, their sibling rivalry went to higher levels and sometimes became physical. Fortunately, Binnie was a lot faster than Frankie who was twice his size. We probably could have had a very successful family sitcom based on our nightly adventures in front of the TV.

There was a time when Frankie accidentally broke the knob that changed the channels (there weren't any remotes in the 1950s). Now we have a dilemma. There is a saying that "necessity in the mother of invention", however, I think it may be better to say that "desperation is the mother of invention." Out of our desperation to change the channels, we invented a solution. First, we used some pliers. Too much work. However, I found out that the key I used to tighten my roller skates did the job.

About a month after my hand got stuck in the fence, my brother Frankie was unfortunately involved in a serious injury. While I was playing nearby with my friends, my brother Binnie came running up to me screaming, "Frankie's hurt...Frankie's hurt!" We ran the short distance back to our apartment, and I saw Frankie with blood dripping from his arm like water from a faucet. We soon found out that Frankie, while chasing someone, fell through a glass door in the entranceway, arms first. It took over 40 stitches to put his skin (what was left of it) back on his arm again.

This is the front entrance of the building.
Directly under the fire escape is where
Frankie ran through the glass door.

• Binnie and the Meatball Machine

Binnie was also a very loving brother. He would often tell me bedtime stories upon request, and most of the time, he would spontaneously create them from his own imagination. One of my favorites was the one about the "Meatball Machine." I laugh as I write this because I don't remember anything about those stories except that I loved them and that the meatball machine was like a machine gun that fired meatballs instead of bullets. Binnie's imagination was quite vivid, and he was a great storyteller.

• **A Close Encounter of the 3rd Kind**

Here is a personal happy story of unexpected excitement that I experienced in 1954. To celebrate my eighth birthday, my parents took me to an Italian restaurant in Manhattan. It was just my mom, my dad, and me. We didn't eat out together often, especially in Manhattan, and this night felt special to me. My parents knew I loved Italian food, and my dad told me that this Italian restaurant was supposed to be one of the best in New York. I know that parents weren't supposed to have favorites, but I'm slowly beginning to realize that I was my parents' favorite.

After sitting down at our traditional Italian restaurant table covered with a red and while checked tablecloth, we ordered our meals of spaghetti and meatballs. Just as a note, I never tasted meatballs and spaghetti in any restaurant that was as good as the one that my Irish mom often cooked. Suddenly, my dad tapped me on the shoulder and said, "Guess who's here?". *Who could it be?* Dad pointed at the table hidden in the corner of the restaurant and said, "Look at that table over there, that's Joe DiMaggio."

I turned around and looked over at this small table, and there he was. I got so excited I almost spat the spaghetti out of my mouth. Dad, equally excited, said, "Why don't you go over there and ask him for an autograph?" I quickly walked over to his table, and went right up to "The Yankee Clipper" (as he was known), and while he was still eating his spaghetti, I said, "Mr. DiMaggio…I am a big fan of yours, and it's my birthday, and I wonder if I can please have your autograph?"

He looked up from his food, with spaghetti still in his mouth, and mumbled, "Sure, kid…Happy Birthday. How old are you? Do you have anything for me to sign?". *Duh…. Why didn't I think of that?* I said, "Mr. DiMaggio, I am eight years old, and I don't have any paper for you to sign." With that, he took out his fancy linen table napkin, laughed, and said, "Sure, kid." He then asked me if I had a pen. *Duh... why didn't I think of that?* Anyway, he took out his own pen and signed the napkin for me writing, "Happy 8th Birthday Kenny. I said, "Thank you," and I smiled and danced my way back to my parents' table.

The story isn't over. I sat down at our table and showed my parents the autograph. Then my dad quickly said, "What about the lady he was with? Did you get her autograph?". "What, lady?" I asked. My dad pointed to a beautiful blonde lady sitting opposite Joe DiMaggio. "Dad... who's that lady?". He smiled and answered, "It's Marilyn Monroe". I think I then said what most eight-year-old baseball fans would have said: "Who's Marilyn Monroe?" I never even noticed that she was there, and even if I did, I wouldn't have known who she was, nor would I have ever thought of asking her to co-sign the napkin. End of story. No, I sadly no longer have that napkin.

- **Jackie Robinson.**

Here is a sports story about an athlete who impacted American History. I was eight years old my dad took me to a game where my new favorite team, the New York Giants, were playing against their arch-rival, the Brooklyn Dodgers. This was my first time watching a game at Ebbets field, the home of the Dodgers. Ebbets field was much smaller than the Giants home field of the Polo grounds, giving it a very intimate feeling.

One of the star players for the Dodgers was Jackie Robinson and this would be the first time that I ever saw him in a live game. In the 3rd inning, Robinson did something that I had never seen a baseball player do before. It is not unusual for a great base runner to steal second base or even third base, but my eyes did not believe what I saw when Robinson stole home base.

The home team fans went crazy. I later found out that he accomplished this rare feat 19 times in his career. Some things you should know. Jackie Robinson, in 1947, became the first black player to ever play professional baseball. He was not the best player in the Negro League, but Dodger owner Branch Rickey believed that Robinson had the best demeanor to withstand the racism that would follow once he put on that Dodger uniform. And he was right.

There are very few people of any color who would have been able to tolerate the pure hatred and bigotry that followed him wherever he played. He and his family even received death threats. Baseball fans, and even those who were not fans, were angered by the loss of their comfort zone of only seeing white baseball players.

It took a few years, but Jackie Robinson soon became a symbol for what is good about America. By breaking the color barrier in baseball, he also became a groundbreaker in eventually improving tensions in our racially torn country.

Jackie Robinson's life story has been made into a feature movie titled "42", which was the number on the back of his baseball jersey. That number, as a tribute to him, has been retired from baseball and no player will ever wear number 42 again. I now have two new baseball heroes to root for. Willie Mays and Jackie Robinson.

Above is a photo of Jackie Robinson accomplishing this rare feat

This next story is difficult to share, but it was a painful part of my life that I will never forget.

- **"Wait until your father gets home."**

"Wait until your father gets home" is an infamous phrase used by comedians when telling jokes about their childhood. Little did I know then that my mom would utter this phrase to me at the most inopportune moment, and it would not at all be funny. I was about nine years old when I got the worst beating of my life.

I had a crush on a girl in my fourth-grade class, and my guess is that she must have felt the same towards me, because she asked me to carry her books and walk her home from school. Unfortunately, she lived further away from my home than I thought. Knowing that I was going to be late, I rushed home and took a shortcut through an empty lot filled with trees and bushes.

In my haste, I stepped on a piece of wood. When I bent down to see why my foot was stuck, I saw a large nail sticking out of my left sneaker. I didn't feel any pain, but I wondered if the nail had gone straight through my foot. I stopped and took off my sneaker to see what damage the nail had inflicted on me, and to my amazement and relief, the nail missed my foot and slid right in between my toes.

That walk took a lot longer than I expected, and instead of arriving home at the usual time of 3:00 PM, I didn't get home until 4:30 PM, just as it was beginning to get dark outside. When I finally got home, my mom was furious with me. She started yelling things like, "Do you know that I called the police. I thought you were hurt or kidnapped?"

As soon as Mom started yelling, I could smell the alcohol on her breath. The fact that she had been drinking only made things worse. Mom went and found a thick belt and began pounding me, with vicious strikes, one after the other. I finally ran away from her and locked myself in the bathroom. When I took off my shirt to assess the damage, I looked in the mirror and couldn't believe the size and redness of the welts on my back that were left by the strap.

It was then that Mom yelled that infamous phrase, "You can hide now, but wait till your father gets home." And I am thinking that the only thing left for my dad to do was to kill me.

Later that evening, Dad came home, and he instantly knew that something was wrong. I was still hiding in the bathroom when I showed him the welts on my back, he walked away angry, but it was not directed at me; it was directed at my mom. A short while later, while I was lying in my bed crying, my dad and mom came up to me and told me that neither one of them would ever hit me again. And they kept that promise.

I was in a state of emotional numbness; however, I do remember wondering how someone I loved and who also loved me could inflict so much pain on me.

• Choose

The argument they had that evening was not the only argument that my parents had. There were too many frequent fights, which, though they were never physical, left an emotional scar that was much deeper and wider than the welts from that strap.

One evening, after one of their fights, I remember Mom and Dad standing together at the front door. My dad had a packed suitcase, and my mom yelled, "And, don't ever come back." My heart sank to the floor. I remember thinking that my world, our family, would never be the same.

A few days later Mom brought me aside and told me that they were going to get a divorce. She told me that Judy wanted to stay with her, and Frankie and Binnie wished to stay with Dad. Mom asked me, "We need you to choose who you want to live with." Wow…my brain was having a difficult time processing all of this.

I looked at my mom with tears in my eyes and said, "I can't choose. I love both of you." She said, "I need you to choose." Then, this angry 10-year-old told my mom, "I cannot choose, and I will not choose. I don't want you to break up."

Of all my siblings, I believe I was the most sensitive. But I don't care how emotionally strong my siblings were; there is no way this break-up could not affect them. Physical scars will eventually heal. Emotional scars, without help, may never heal. The thought that my parents were getting a divorce triggered old abandonment issues, but what made it even worse was, at that age, I was unable to identify the origins of my pain and confusion about why they were breaking up. Was it my fault?

About a week later Dad returned home, and all thoughts of them getting divorced had become either silent or non-existent. Though mom's drinking continued, as well as their arguments, they stayed together. To this day, I'm not sure which would have been mentally healthier for me and my siblings in terms of whether they should have divorced or stayed together as they did. This type of emotional trauma is difficult to articulate, except to say that it left a hole in my soul, wondering who is going to take care of me, and again, was it my fault.

About a month later, I wrote in chalk on the red brick wall outside the lobby door of our apartment building, "I hate my father." I don't remember the exact moment that triggered this outburst, but I probably wrote this because my mom and dad were arguing daily, and I sided with my mom. Maybe, it was because I was still angry about those years when my dad was in Korea.

It was just a few days later my dad took me outside and pointed to what I had written on the wall, and he asked me if I had written it. I reluctantly told him, "Yes." *I was afraid he would hit me.* I remember seeing tears in my dad's eyes, and this was the first time I ever saw him cry. He told me that he was sorry and that he promised to be a better dad. He then held me tightly in his arms, and we both cried together. He was true to his words, and not only did he become a better dad, but he also became my best friend.

CHAPTER SIX

Television, Music & Movies (1951-1955)

- **Television**

Time for a change of pace.

My brothers and I spent way too many hours in front of the TV. By 1951, over 12 million people in the US owned TV sets, representing a significant increase from the 6,000 TV sets sold in 1946. This illustrates the tremendous impact that the medium of television had on our American way of life. The sitcom, *I Love Lucy*, is still a big hit and it was on at the perfect time for Mom to watch it after coming home from work. This show remained one of the most popular TV shows for over the next thirty years.

Television was still a relatively new phenomenon, and most, if not all, TV shows were 'live' and variety shows were in front of a live audience. One of our favorite family evening shows was the *Dean Martin and Jerry Lewis Show*. My mom's favorites included the *Jimmy Durante Show*, the *Dinah Shore Show*, and the *Lawrence Welk Music Show*. Most of these were comedy and variety shows. It must have been an extremely rare occasion for my dad to watch TV with all of us. He was too busy working.

Other very popular shows that we watched included the *Texaco Star Theater*, starring comedian Milton Berle (also known as Uncle

Miltie), and *Your Show of Shows*, starring comedian Sid Caesar. I also have a vivid memory of our new RCA television. It was located right in the corner of the living room of our Forest Hills apartment. My brothers and I had a great view of the TV when we often peeked around the open bedroom door after we were sent to bed. If my parents ever turned their heads in our direction, which happened a few times, they would see our three heads, one on top of the other, trying to watch TV.

My sister, Judy, was not so lucky because her bedroom was on the other side of the apartment, and I doubt that she ever got the benefits that my brothers and I shared in cheating on our bedtime.

       Lucille Ball and Dezi Arnaz   Our 1952 RCA TV set

Saturday morning television was devoted to kids. There was the *Howdy Doody Show* (one of my favorites), with colorful characters including Buffalo Bob (Smith), Clarabelle the Clown, Phineas T. Bluster, and a very pretty Indian lady called Princess Summerfall - Winterspring. There were also Saturday morning cartoons, including *Mickey Mouse, Tom and Jerry, Elmer Fudd,* and *Sylvester the Cat.*

One of my favorite afternoon shows was *Flash Gordon,* a science fiction fantasy whose primitive graphics looked very real to a six-year-old. Another daily daytime show, *The Lone Ranger,* captured the imaginations of the young American public. At a time when racism was still a large part of our culture, *The Lone Ranger* show was the first national TV show to have a native American Indian actor, Jay

Silverheels, as the co-star. His character was the Lone Ranger's side-kick, Tonto.

Tonto made the phrase "Kemosabe" famous whenever he referred to the Lone Ranger (actor Clayton Moore). Kimosabe, translated, means trusted friend. My young friends and I would often borrow this phrase when talking to each other. "Hey, Kimosabe, do you want to go play baseball?"

The Lone Ranger and Tonto   **Buffalo Bob and Howdy Doody**

• **Music**

With the ever-increasing popularity of television, listening to the radio for most American families became somewhat obsolete. In the '40s and early '50s the radio was the exclusive form of home entertainment. By the mid-50s, the radio was rarely used in the household and mostly listened to while in a car.

Whether we were listening to the radio or watching TV, music in the early 50s, still had its share of great vocalists, such as Nat King Cole, Tony Bennett, Perry Como, Dinah Shore, The Andrews Sisters, Rosemary Clooney, Dean Martin, Frank Sinatra, and Andy Williams.

Rock ' n ' roll had not yet affected (or some may say 'infected') the American youth until 1954, when a Cleveland radio disc jockey, Alan Freed, introduced various rock n ' roll songs on his radio show. Alan Freed then moved from Cleveland to New York City, and the rest is history. Alan Freed is also credited for coining the phrase "Rock n Roll".

In 1946, Arthur Crudup recorded "That's All Right Mama," which received very little airtime. However, in 1954, Elvis Presley re-recorded it and it became a huge hit. Most historians agree that the song "Rocket 88" (1951) by Jackie Brenston (Ike Turner) and his Delta Cats should receive credit for being the first hit Rock n Roll song. The rock 'n roll songs I grew up with did not arrive until 1955, when a slew of recording artists had numerous hit records.

- **Movies**

Saturday afternoons were memorable. My parents did not argue every minute of every day, and some days seemed 'normal'. On Saturdays, Mom would often send the four of us to the movies, to give herself time to relax. There were two movie theaters, within walking distance, and they were located around the corner from each other.

One of the theaters was called "The Midway," and the name of the other theater was the "Loews." Frankie, who was about 10 years old at the time, would lead us on a 9-block walk to movie theater and cartoon heaven. It was not unusual for us to get there around 11 AM and stay until about 5 or 6 PM. The movie tickets cost about 65 cents each, and we would watch two movies (billed as a 'double-header'). And, if it were 'cartoon Saturday, there would also be 15 – 20 consecutive cartoons. I'm unsure how much popcorn and candy we ate, but I know it was more than we should have.

My first recollection of going to the movies was with my siblings when we watched the very scary *House of Wax* (1953) starring Vincent Price. However, the movie that gave me the most nightmares was *The Mummy*, starring movie actor Boris Karloff. This movie was initially released in 1932, way before I was born, but I clearly remember seeing it on TV when I was about seven years old. I also remember my brothers, Frankie and Binnie, wrapping themselves up, using toilet paper, like mummies, walking and stalking into our bedroom late at night just to scare me. It worked.

Frankie could have been a good actor, as shown by the way he walked to my bed, slowly dragging his left foot behind him. He was very convincing while walking and making some inaudible scary sounds. I remember lying in bed with my head under the pillow, praying for someone to help me out of this bad dream that I was having while I was still awake.

I also recall watching the original movie *A Night to Remember,* at the Midway Theater. This movie was about the sinking of the Titanic. Another movie that put me in awe was *20,000 Leagues Under the Sea,* based on the novel written by Jules Verne. The reason this movie was so memorable was that it was the first movie I ever saw that was in Technicolor. Another movie that was also in color was *The King and I,* which first appeared as a Broadway Play in New York City. This movie and play made an instant star of the leading man, Yul Brynner. I now wondered if 'color' TV far behind?

One of the most popular movies, *A Place in the Sun* (1951), marked the breakthrough debut of future megastar Elizabeth Taylor. Then there was *A Streetcar Named Desire* (1951), again a breakthrough performance for another megastar, Marlon Brando (of Godfather fame). I honestly don't remember seeing these two films when they were released in theaters; however, I did see all of them on television at a later time.

The popularity of Marlon Brando and James Dean and the acting roles they had, led to a change in the way Americans dressed. Men and women would soon be wearing the more comfortable and casual pants called 'jeans. In the 1950s, we called them dungarees. This was a drastic change in our culture. People who are used to wearing dressy clothes to go to events and church are now wearing jeans. We are now beginning to see that the world is slowly changing.

You will soon read about our summers from 1951 to 1954, which provided their own source of family fun when we started going to the Catskills.

Boris Karloff as the 'Mummy', And the source of too many nightmares

CHAPTER SEVEN

Early Summers (1951 – 1954)

- **The Catskills**

From 1951 to 1954, we spent our entire summer months in the Catskill Mountains. The Catskill mountain range is located approximately 100 miles north of New York City. This region of numerous hotels and bungalow colonies, and of course beautiful mountains, was also known as the Jewish Alps and/or the Borscht Belt. It's main visitors were Jewish families from New York City. Here is an oddity. The Catskills, like 'The' Bronx, needs the word 'The' as part of their title. No one ever says, "I'm going to Catskills or I'm going to Bronx", it just doesn't sound right. Strange, huh? And no one would ever say, "I'm going to The Manhattan." They would say, "I'm going to Manhattan."

My dad, in addition to giving piano lessons in all five boroughs of New York, throughout the school year, was also a band leader in some of the Catskills' resorts during the summer. Unlike the other months, Dad was more available to our family than ever before. His summer job included doing just four shows a week. That plus the rehearsals only added up to an average of working just four hours a day. Not bad for him and it was great for us.

The 120-mile car trip from NYC usually took about 2 ½ hours, depending on traffic. Summer vacation usually started on the July 4th weekend when the New York weather was hot and humid. Quite often, because of the summer heat, too many cars overheated on the highway (NY State Thruway) on the way up to the Catskills, and this drive it could take as long as 3 – 4 hours to get to the hotels from New York City.

Our car and almost every other car in the early '50s, did not have air conditioning. This often made the trip unbearable on a hot day, especially with four kids piled into the back seat of a 1949 Plymouth.

A 1949 Plymouth very similar to our car.

Although the heat and humidity were an inconvenience for our long trip, it was, however, never boring. The scenery of the multi-colored trees and mountains was breathtaking. The four of us would often sing songs in the back of the car, eventually causing our dad to turn on the radio to help drown out our off-key voices. We also played games like counting all the blue cars that we could see on the trip. Another game we also played was twenty-one questions. These games helped make a long trip that much shorter and more fun.

In the summers of 1951, 52, and 53, my dad was the band leader at three different hotels. The staff who worked at the hotel were not allowed to stay there because they needed their rooms for their guests. Because of this our family would stay in a nearby bungalow colony.

- **Bungalow Colonies**

Those two words, bungalow colony, must sound very weird to anyone who does not know what they are. A bungalow colony was a group (7 – 15) of very small single-story cottages that had 1-3 small bedrooms, a kitchen, and a small bathroom with a shower and toilet.

You can imagine how tight the living conditions were for a family of six like ours. There was little to no privacy for anyone. In our third summer (1953) my dad became the band leader at the beautiful Evans Hotel.

The Evans Hotel and its nearby surroundings, including Kiamesha Lake.

To me, this hotel was majestic. It had two swimming pools, tennis courts, a theater for nighttime entertainment, a large dining room, acres of land, and a fantastic view of the local mountains and scenery.

- **Tannersville**

When Dad was working at the Evan's Hotel, we stayed in a bungalow colony in a small town called Tannersville, which was almost a one-hour drive away from the hotel. This was a long commute for my dad to go to work, but I'm sure he had a good reason.

Our bungalow in Tannersville had a large living room and kitchen area, as well as three bedrooms. The entire property consisted of about ten bungalows, each occupied by Jewish families spending their summer vacation. I can still picture that the colony had approximately 10-20 acres of land, which was not well-maintained, and it had thick grass growing everywhere.

Our bungalow is the one in the middle with a back porch.
Someone must had cut the grass for the photo, HA!

It is here where I learned how to play baseball. When it was sunny, which was almost every day, my brother Frankie would hit fly balls to all the kids into those deep-weeded fields, and I soon perfected my skills as an outfielder. Fly balls were always an adventure when about eight of us tried to catch the same fly ball. We were pushing and shoving while falling over each other with each of us shouting simultaneously, "I got it. I got it". It's kind of funny that it was rare for anyone to ever 'get it'. Still, we were having a great time.

Taken at the Tannersville bungalow colony. In the back are Frankie (left) then Binnie. I am in front of Frankie next to Judy

• The Incredible Water

One of my most vivid memories of that summer in Tannersville was the spring water. This spring was like a mini river, but only about six feet wide, with a constant downhill flow of water over numerous rocks. This spring was just a couple of hundred yards from our bungalow and located in the woods about 100 feet from a country road.

We, of course, had a kitchen with running hot and cold water, but the water from this spring was special. Every day the four of us would bring as many one-gallon glass jugs as we could carry and we would fill them with the freezing cold spring water and bring them back to the bungalow. I am describing this simply because this was, and remains, the best-tasting water I have ever had in my entire life.

I know it is a common belief that water has no flavor or taste but believe me when I tell you that this spring water had an indescribable flavor, and it was always ice cold. Many years ago, I was reminiscing with my 95-year-old dad about our stay in Tannersville, and the first words out of his mouth were, "Do you remember the taste of the spring water?". I hope this proves my point.

If someone from the future had come back and told me that one day we would be paying for water, and it would come in plastic (or glass) bottles, I would have thought they were crazy. It shouldn't be a surprise that the bottled water companies of today often advertise that they use 'spring' water.

Another great memory was our numerous visits to the nearby small town of Tannersville, which had a movie theater, a small grocery store, and a lake. At the lake, we would spend countless hours swimming and rowing boats and having a great time. A few months before the summer, my brother Frankie rebuilt a rowboat at home, towed it up to the lake and put a small Edson motor on it—great memories and fun. Nights at the bungalow colony were also memorable, and were often spent around a campfire, where we would roast hot dogs and marshmallows, tell ghost stories, and sing country and cowboy songs. Life is good.

The night sky provided a breathtaking view of the stars. Being over 100 miles away from any major city, there was no air pollution or city lights to obstruct this amazing view. This recent memory of seeing countless stars as they were meant to be seen motivated me to take my wife (Vita) and my two sons (Kevin & Chris) to spend four days at Yosemite National Park.

•   **Who is Nat Rand?**

During one of our summer family visits to the Evan's hotel, I walked near the stage while my dad was playing, and I noticed that each member of his seven-piece orchestra had a cardboard poster in front of their chairs with the name "The Nat Rand Orchestra." *Hmmm? Who is Nat Rand, my last name is Temsky?* When I asked my dad, he told me that 'Rand' was his 'stage' name, and the next day he gave me a lesson in American history and politics. I am eight years old, and I know and care nothing about history or politics. However, I would soon learn a valuable lesson.

In 1950, Senator Joe McCarthy, a Republican from Wisconsin, launched a campaign against communism and alleged spies throughout the US government. McCarthy's paranoia did not stop there as he was quick to add any of his critics of his beliefs to his list, and he even went on to attack Jewish entertainers as communist sympathizers. Soon after, McCarthy also went after homosexuals. He continued, unstopped, on a two-year mission and witch hunt to try and expose American communists. McCarthy, in his efforts to scare the public and gather support, also started a rumor that the fluoride in our drinking water was a communist plot.

To avoid McCarthy's anti-Semitic persecution, many entertainers would unofficially change their last names (which were Jewish) to names that were more mainstream in America. Among the actors and entertainers who changed their original Jewish names were Tony Curtis, Kirk Douglas, Edward G. Robinson, Rock Hudson, Jerry Lewis, Nat Rand, and many more.

During the McCarthy hearings (1954), the senator was eventually humiliated as an overzealous, paranoid patriot who was intent on promoting himself at the cost of destroying the lives of decent people. He is the first senator to be admonished by the US Senate.

In another page from history, from 1951 to 1953, the famous spy trial against Julius and Ethel Rosenberg began and ended in a conviction that led to their execution. This trial received major headlines, and our country was split over the possible guilt or innocence of this married couple. The Rosenberg's were Jewish and could very well have been the victims of McCarthyism and the perceived, "communist threat."

• Summers in the Catskills

Those early summers in the Catskills are among my fondest memories while growing up in the 1950s. Staying in those bungalow colonies and our times at the hotels were 100 times better than going to a sleepaway camp for a week, which is what many of our friends from home would often do.

Labor Day weekend, which marked the end of summer vacation, was soon approaching, and it was sad to see this summer in Tannersville come to an end. In the summer of 1954, my dad became the band leader at the prestigious Brown's Hotel. His tenure at this hotel lasted for about 30 years, and our family spent about 14 summers there.

Looking back, that summer in Tannersville was as good as it could get. So many memories. So many good times. It was like being in a two-month camp where every single day was magical. There are so many stories to tell, and I have saved them for you in the upcoming chapters. We would soon move into a new apartment, bringing with it some new adventures. My rollercoaster ride of life would continue.

BREAKING NEWS (1951 – 1954)

Did You Know that….

- **In 1951**, Harry Truman was still President.
- The United States population has now grown to 151 million, with an average life expectancy of 68 years.
- Congress passed the 22nd Amendment, which limited presidents to two terms. This was a direct result of Franklin D. Roosevelt's (FDR) winning four consecutive presidential elections.
- **In 1952**, Dwight Eisenhower was elected president
- The first hydrogen bomb was detonated by the U.S.
- **In 1953** there was the coronation of Queen Elizabeth I
- **In 1954**, In a landmark decision (Brown vs. Board of Education), The US Supreme Court declared state-segregation in public schools unconstitutional
- *Roger Bannister became the first person to run a mile in under four minutes, a major athletic achievement.

Famous people born in this period:

- **1946:** Sylvester Stallone, Cher, Reggie Jackson, Dolly Parton, Donald Trump, Bill Clinton and Lisa Minelli
- **1947**: Kareem Abdul-Jabbar, Hillary Clinton, Arnold Schwarzenegger,
- **1948**: Billy Crystal, Samuel Jackson, James Taylor, Al Gore.
- **1949:** Lionel Richie, George Foreman, Richard Gere,
- **1950:** Stevie Wonder, Marilyn Monroe
- *1951: Robin Williams, Phil Collins, Dale Earnhardt, and Sting

THE COST OF LIVING

	1951	1954
• New House	$ 9,000	$10,500
• Avg. Income	$ 3,515	$ 4,137
• New Car	$ 1,520	$ 1,910
• Average Rent	$78/m	$ 87/m
• Movie Ticket	65 ℂ	75 ℂ
• Gasoline	9 ℂ/gal.	23 c/gal
• Postage stamp	3 ℂ	3 ℂ

FOOD

	1951	1954
• Sugar	85 ℂ/ 10 lbs.	85ℂ/ 10 lbs.
• Milk	929ℂ/ gal.	92ℂ/ gal.
• Coffee	72ℂ/ pound	80ℂ/ pound
• Bacon	52ℂ/ pound	58ℂ/ pound
• Eggs	24ℂ/ dozen	27ℂ/dozen
• Hamburger	50ℂ/pound	56ℂ/ pound
• Loaf of Bread	16 ℂ/ each	18ℂ/ each

Part III: 1955 – 1958

CHAPTER EIGHT

Walden Terrace

It is1955, while still living in Forest Hills, we moved into a brand-new apartment complex called Walden Terrace. This apartment complex was approximately a mile from our previous apartment, and the apartment buildings were all white, giving them an elegant appearance. Our new apartment was even larger than our previous one, and it had an elegant sunken living room which was a couple of steps down from the dining room.

To me, our apartment was something that you would only see on TV. A sunken living room, Wow! We also had a small outdoor patio (or porch). Our apartment was located on the first floor, which provided us with a great view of the tree-lined street through the large window in the living room.

The Walden Terrace complex consisted of two blocks of apartments, with approximately six buildings per block, and each apartment building was eight stories tall. These buildings stood out as one of the highest structures in the growing community of Forest Hills. I have numerous memories of our time living in these new apartments, and I hope I can recall most of them.

The Walden Terrace Apartments

(1956), Mom and Dad are sitting down. In the Back row left to right,
are me (10), Frankie (a mature 13), Judy (9), and Binnie (12).

It appears that we are one big happy family, and for the most
part, we were, however, things may not always be what they seem,
as you will soon learn. This photo must have been taken on a special

occasion. Notice that we are all dressed up and dad is wearing a tuxedo. I don't remember why.

• A New School

When I finished sixth grade, my parents were given the option to allow me to skip seventh grade and proceed directly to eighth grade. This was the result of my high scores in math and science on national tests. However, I was already the youngest student in all of my grade levels, and my parents didn't think that it would be a wise decision for my social growth to skip a grade.

My new school was Halsey Junior High School and was located two blocks away from my previous elementary school. Once the school year began, I quickly made new friends and for the first time, I started to enjoy going to school.

Looking back, the education system in the 1950s and 1960s differed significantly from the one we have today. For example, when I was in elementary school and junior high school, I remember that the standard curriculum had us taking classes in art and music. I find it disheartening that today's students may know nothing about the greats in classical music, such as Beethoven, Bach, and Mozart. The same applies to the great artists such as Da Vinci, Picasso, and Michelangelo.

I also remember the joy of taking 'shop' classes, such as woodworking, ceramics, and mechanical drawing. Again, these were required classes from the curriculum. These classes taught us how to work in teams and helped prepare us for the 'real' world. About 30 years ago, many schools across the country eliminated these classes from their curricula due to budgetary reasons.

We also had those school-sponsored field trips. One month, we would spend a day at the Empire State Building, the next month, we would visit the Statue of Liberty, and there were too many other trips to remember them all. Learning became fun.

I was recently shocked to hear that public schools are no longer teaching penmanship and cursive writing. It's just sad that an entire form of communication is now disappearing. Although technology is supposedly moving us forward, it is also taking away 'intimacy' in our efforts to communicate with each other. Most of our communication today is through texting and emailing. Yes, it saves time and is much faster, but it does lack intimacy. I guess we can always add some emojis.

Unfortunately, the English language today, is being reduced to three, and four-letter acronyms such as FYI and LMAO. Pretty soon, we will no longer speak in sentences. Yes. I plead guilty. I also use 'OMG' when writing on the classroom board and 'LMAO' when texting with friends. However, I can write a complete sentence, and I can recognize the names of Bach, Mozart, Da Vinci, and Rembrandt, and appreciate their genius. As a teacher I believe in a holistic approach to education. I never once thought that my sole objective was just to teach mathematics. I wanted to teach my students how to collaborate and how to 'think'. Back to some fun.

- **Stoopball (what's that?)**

Stoopball is a sports game phenomenon typically played by kids in NYC or those living in apartment buildings (or townhouses), that have steps leading to the front door and lobby. To play this game we used a Spalding rubber ball, and it had to be a Spalding ball because they were the best. The objective was to throw the ball hard against the stoop (step), and if we made good contact, the ball would fly over the street, where the opposing team would try to catch it in mid-air.

Any ball caught in the air was, of course, an out. The trick was to be lucky or skillful enough to throw the ball directly at the curve of the stoop where it had a sharper edge. The ball would then fly twice as far and fast, likely becoming an automatic home run. In the Spring and Summer, we spent many hours playing stoopball, but it was our way of having innocent and safe fun. Sometimes it wasn't safe because street traffic often interrupted our game.

Here is the entrance to our apartment building and
the three steps (stoops) leading to the lobby.

• Coney Island, New York

My dad seemed to have a knack for surprising me with something special on my birthdays, and he did so again on my ninth
birthday when he brought me to the Coney Island Amusement Park
and beach in Brooklyn, New York. It was only dad and me on this
special day at Coney Island.

My birthday, being in late April, was not always accompanied
by the best weather. On this day, it was cloudy and relatively cold,
so going to the beach was not an option. However, there was still
this incredible Amusement Park to see and enjoy. Of course, there
also was the world-famous Nathan's hot dog stand (store). Since
1972, Nathan's has hosted an annual nationally televised July 4th hot
dog-eating contest. Joey Chestnut has won this contest 16 times and
set the world record in 2020 for eating 75 hot dogs in 10 minutes.
My personal record is eating four hot dogs. However, my record for
eating pancakes is significantly higher (a story for later).

The world famous Nathan's at Coney Island.

The amusement park had some very unique rides. Their roller-coaster, named the Cyclone, was, at that time, the fastest in the world, reaching a speed of 99 miles per hour. This ride was unforgettable even for an adventurous and risk-taking nine-year-old. And there was this other ride called the Steeplechase which featured Merry-Go-Round-style horses on an elevated racetrack circling (racing) around a building. What you can't see in the photo below is that the wooden beams in between the horses were not there when I went on this ride.

The Steeple Chase   The Cyclone

The empty space between the horses scared me like no other ride I had ever been on. I was in constant fear of falling through the opening to the ground about 20 feet below. I rode the Cyclone roller-coaster three times, but I only rode the steeplechase ride once. Once was enough for me. I am lucky I didn't soil my pants.

A few minutes later my dad and I walked over to the Coney Island Parachute Jump. This structure was an exhibit built for the World's Fair in 1939, and it stood 262 feet high. The elevator ride to the top wasn't too bad, except for the anticipation of what was soon to happen. At the top, my dad and I were strapped into a ski lift-type chair. There were no cushions, just a bar across our laps and handle-bars on our sides.

The attendant at the top soon said, "One, Two, Three," and the unexpected happened. When the parachute was released, we were both suspended in mid-air off of the chair. I thought I was going to die. It seems that for someone so young I experienced my share of life and death experiences (*and I am just beginning*). We were at least 6 inches above our chairs. What was probably just a few seconds of being lifted off our chair seemed like an eternity for me. Of course, we made it safely down, but this time, I think I did soil my pants (just kidding).

The Coney Island Parachute Jump.

Recently, my wife and I happened to watch the Academy Award-winning movie 'Anora', and to my pleasant surprise, a scene in the film showed Coney Island and the rides I have just mentioned. This brought back so many great memories, including my fear of dying that day. It was sad to learn that this Amusement Park had recently closed in 2023. Sometimes, if you live long enough, parts of your history disappear and are lost forever, except for memories which are forever forged into our life experiences.

Though my dad and I have been to Coney Island many times since my birthday, our primary purpose was to eat hot dogs—going on rides were a second option. I do, however, still miss the (much safer) bumper cars.

- **The World is Changing**

Though my own interests are focused on family, friends, and sports; between studying current events in school and reading newspaper headlines, I was not totally clueless about what was going on in the world, and I was partially fascinated by the concept of the "Cold War" and the "Race to Space." When I read the newspaper, I would always start with back pages, for two reasons. One was that was where they had the sports section, the other reason was that the headlines on the front page were often scary as it often referred to the 'Cold War' between Russia and the United States or some other tragic events.

Although Russia and the U.S. were allies during World War II (1939-1945), we soon became bitter rivals. In contrast to fighting with guns and bombs, our two countries became enemies in terms of each of our political and economic ideologies (aka The Cold War).

Part of this Cold War was the 'race to space,' where both countries were in fierce competition to be the first to reach space and land on the moon. In October of 1957, Russia successfully launched a series of satellites (Sputnik) into space, giving them a huge propaganda boost and bragging rights. After several failed attempts, the U.S. finally launched its own satellite, Explorer One, in January of 1958

In 1955, another significant event captured the nation's attention. Rosa Parks, a woman of color, was arrested for refusing to give up her seat on a public bus in Montgomery, Alabama. Her defiance and her courageous act triggered others to protest what was known as 'Jim Crow' laws, and many credit her for igniting the civil rights movement. Inspired by her protest, black Americans began to test the culture of racism all throughout our country.

The above events were the catalyst for significant changes in how we lived, but perhaps we should move on to some more fun times and memories. Now back to our regular programming.

- **A "Brand New Car"**

I was ten years old when my dad came to pick me up from my school. It was probably late November, because I remember it was already getting dark outside by late afternoon. The streetlamp light was on, and I could see the snow fluttering through the light. Directly below that streetlamp was a brand-new 1956 two-tone gray Chevy with white-wall tires. This incident had very little significance, except that it reaffirmed in my mind that we were economically doing okay, and it was the first time I recalled that we had ever owned a new car. I was not sad to say goodbye to our old 1949 Plymouth.

Our 1956 two-tone Chevy

Also in 1956, Ford came out with its competition for the Corvette, called the Ford Thunderbird. It's release price was $3548. You can buy this classic car now for $30,000 - $70,000.

A 1956 Ford Thunderbird

- **Party Time**

I made many friends at our new location, some of them lived in our apartment complex, but most of my new friends were my classmates from JHS. We were way too young to date, but we would frequently host parties on Friday or Saturday evenings at various homes, including mine. I remember dancing to the latest songs and playing some of the games that pre-teens played.

Yes, we played the kissing game, "spin the bottle". I wonder how many readers remember playing that fun game. It was a great way to snatch a kiss from someone you had a crush on. Another game we played was called "lights out". In this game, we turned off all of the lights, leaving the living room totally dark. Someone was in charge of the phonograph and would start and stop the music at unannounced intervals.

The game began with a girl on a guy's lap, and when the music stopped, the girl would switch to a new lap. There was a lot of kissing, and trust me, it was nothing but innocent fun. Great times. I can't say I miss them because my wife will read this book. No, we never played this game while our parents were home. They trusted us and they weren't crazy about listening to listen to Rock 'n' Roll music.

- **Cousin Albert and Binnie**

Cousin Albert

It was around 1955 when my dad told us that we were direct descendants of Albert Einstein. My dad's great-grandfather (Jaklob Einstein) was the first cousin of Albert Einstein, which made my dad the third cousin of Albert Einstein.

Dad has told us many stories of him meeting Einstein at family gatherings, including one when they played a duet together. Einstein played the violin. Einstein's genes may also have played a role in my brother Binnie's career choice to be an engineer, as well as my choice to become a mathematics instructor.

Binnie

After graduating from college, Binnie was recruited by Grumman Aircraft. His assignment was to create an electrical fail-safe system for the first Apollo mission. I am proud to say that my brother's name, James 'Binnie' Rand, is on a plaque on the moon along with the other engineers who worked on this mission. Me? I went on to teach mathematics on a variety of levels, from JHS to University, for a total of 47 years.

- **Terror…Sheer Terror!**

The year is 1957. We were still living in Walden Terrace in Forest Hills, and I believe I was eleven years old. I was sitting in our living room playing with some paper clips and rubber bands, trying to see how far I could shoot the paper clip using the rubber band. It seems like I am always practicing my aim.

As I was doing this; I looked out the living room window and noticed a delivery boy bringing some groceries. He was no more than 8 feet away and was walking down the ramp to the basement of my apartment building. Well, my athletic instincts took over, and I devised the stupid idea of aiming at a 'live' target, and I let one rip.

This is the walkway down to the basement, where the delivery boy was walking. My stupid shot came from the living room window above the railing on the right side.

This incident ranks as one of the dumbest things I've ever done in my entire life. The paper clip hit the delivery boy in the back of his neck and drew instant blood. Afraid to see the consequences of my actions, I ducked down as fast as I could and hid underneath the window. A minute later, I peeked up and noticed my brother, Binnie, walking towards the entrance to our building.

A minute later, Binnie opened the front door of our apartment, saw me hiding under the window, and said the words that would cause endless sleepless nights for the following year. He said, "Why is that Gang member trying to look into our windows?" *Gang member? Are you kidding me?* I didn't just hit any ordinary delivery boy. I hit a member of the infamous Corona Dukes.

Binnie quickly closed the curtains to prevent the gang member from looking into the apartment. He then continued to scare the living daylight out of me by telling me that I was "toast" and I would be lucky to live another day. He said, "Are you crazy? How could you do that?" I asked him how he knew the kid was a gang member, and he said he could see that he was wearing a garrison belt (two-inch-wide black belt) with a C.D. (Corona Dukes) carved on it.

This gang was from an area in Queens (about 2 miles from our apartment) called Corona, and they were by far the most feared gang in all of Queens, if not all of NYC. Although Forest Hills was a very safe community with little or no crime. I was afraid to leave our apartment, and I stayed home the next day, faking some incurable illness, which, fortunately, my parents believed. Still, I knew that I eventually would have to leave our apartment and hopefully find a way to avoid my upcoming death by stabbing.

I managed to live through the next few weeks, but there wasn't a single day or evening when I didn't live in fear. I toyed with the idea that if I got caught, I would confront him and tell him the truth by simply confessing and apologizing, but my brother said that the gang member might not be merciful, and if he was, then he would only stab me once and not multiple times.

A few weeks later, my friends and I were walking home from the movie theater, when we stopped in a small grocery store on 108th St. And guess who was there? So now I know where he worked, and I also now know "exactly" what he looked like. He was short, about 5'5", and had a pockmarked face and a knife scar on his left cheek. He looked just like a character from the movie *West Side Story.* The good news is that he did not recognize me, but I couldn't leave that store fast enough.

A few weeks after that, I was playing with some friends down the street; we were no more than 100 feet away from my apartment, and guess who drove up on his bicycle? *Oh shit. I am dead. This is it.* He came right up to us and asked, "Do any of you know who lives in that apartment over there?" Pointing, of course, up the street towards my apartment. *Oh shit. I'm going to die today.*

Meanwhile, I know that my friends know where I live, so now, I am just praying. Before my friends could say anything, I quickly answered, "What apartment? Where? Can you show it to me?" Already knowing the answers, I did this to get away from my friends, who would more than likely contribute to my upcoming death. I walked up the street with the gang member, with my knees knocking against each other.

We soon stood right in front of my apartment window. He said, "This one here," and he pointed to my apartment. I lied and said, "No, I don't know who lives there," and asked him, "Why?" He said, "No special reason," and then he took off. Can you even begin to imagine the internal fear I was going through? Again… This was sheer terror for me for the next few months. I knew I was going to die but I didn't know when it would eventually happen. Months passed without any further incident. This was about the time I became religious, praying every day that this would not be the day I died.

Then, one day, I received life-changing news from my parents: we were going to move from Forest Hills to upstate New York. I couldn't believe it. Maybe I wasn't going to die after all. Get ready for the bizarre ending to this story.

The day we moved, as we were leaving our apartment, carrying boxes to our car, and closing our front door for the last time, the gang member just happened to be standing there no more than 10 feet away. He was about to get on the elevator to make a grocery delivery to another apartment. He looked straight at me, and the look on his face said, *"You are a dead kid."*

Once he got in the elevator, I ran to our car, never to see or be seen by him again. Adios, Forest Hills, hello, Westchester, NY. Finally, I was able to sleep again.

At the end of the hallway is our front door
On the near right is the blue door of the elevator.

From Zero to Hero

I need to take a short step back in time.

At the age of nine years old, I am eligible to start playing Little League baseball. My brother Frankie (12 years old) also played and was probably the biggest and best on our team. Having an athletic and talented brother didn't help because I was terrible. I sucked. And I was awful for another two years. Over a period of three years, I think I struck out every time I went up to bat. I was lucky to even hit a foul ball.

For over two years, I had zero hits... until the very last game of my third year, when I finally connected (yes, there are miracles), and I hit a deep fly ball to right field. The ball rolled forever, and I made an "inside the park" home run. YAY. Not only did I get my first hit, but I hit a home run.

My little league career would soon take a drastic turn. In the beginning of summer (1957) I am about 5'4" and eleven years old when we went upstate to Brown's Hotel in late June. When summer vacation was over, we left the hotel and arrived home the day after Labor Day. Upon entering our Forest Hills apartment, I walked through the door, looked around, and all the furniture seemed smaller than it was went we left for vacation. Hmmm? The bed in my room seemed to be a lot further from my eyes. It used to be as high as my knee, but now it was only ½ way up my shin. Even the sink and toilet in the bathroom seemed closer to the floor.

None of my old clothes fit anymore. I did not realize it, but I grew about five inches during the summer and was now about 5'9". I am not sure if that is even physically possible?

Wow, what a growing spurt, and it was a pleasant surprise. I am now the tallest in the family, and I looked down at my two older brothers and both of my parents. I was also stronger and I could hit a baseball a lot further; my increase in height also helped when I first started learning how to play basketball. I grew another two inches the following year, but strangely enough, that was the end of it. I reached the peak of my height and growth spurt at the age of 13. How sad. I never grew another inch, at least vertically.

Back to my last year of Little League. I am 12 years old and everything changed and I now dwarfed every kid in the little league. And through some divine intervention, I was now the best ball player in the league. I am unsure how it happened, but in my last year of Little League (1958), I didn't strike out, not once. I even remember my stats. I went 20 for 32. That's a .628 batting average and I hit 4 Home Runs. I played center field (like my hero Willie Mays) and threw out four runners at home or on the base paths.

I was even able to "call" one of my Home Runs. There was one game where we were losing by one run, and we were down to our last out in the bottom of the seventh and last inning. I approached my teammate and confidently told him that if he got on base, I would hit a home run. Well, guess what? He drew a walk, and then I hit a home run to left-center field, and we won the game. Move over, Babe Ruth. Enough bragging for now.

Now, Get Ready for this Incredible Story

It's April 25th, 1958, and it is my 12th birthday. My dad came home early from work and told me we were going out to dinner to celebrate my birthday. Dad had done this before (on another memorable birthday), so there was nothing unusual about this except that it seemed to take forever (about 1 ½ hours) for us to reach our destination. When we finally left the highway, I noticed a sign that said we had arrived in Philadelphia. *Philadelphia?* We soon parked the car and walked a few blocks, and then it hit me.

Directly in front of us was Connie Mack Stadium, where the Phillies played their home games. I knew right then what my birthday gift was. Dad was taking me to watch the Giants (and my hero Willie Mays) play the Phillies that night. This would be the Giants' first trip back to the East Coast after the team had moved to San Francisco. I cannot put into words how I felt. It was like a dream come true, but this dream was not over yet.

We arrived at the stadium one hour early, and the Giants were on the field, having fielding and batting practice. Our great box seats were about three rows behind the end of the 3rd base (Giants) dugout. About 15 minutes later, Willie Mays, after finishing his warmups, started to head for the Giants' dugout.

A swarm of kids ran from their seats to the dugout, shouting, "Willie, please sign my baseball. "Please sign my glove." My dad said, "Why don't you go down there and try to get his autograph?" I told my dad that I did not have anything for him to sign. Dad then pulled out a brand-new major-league baseball from his coat and gave it to me. Lucky me. I quickly ran down to the railing near the dugout, as dozens of kids (my competition) screamed, "Willie, Willie, can I have an autograph?"

At that time, I thought the chances of me getting an autograph were about 'zero to none.' Suddenly, Willie Mays got closer to the railing and shouted, "Is there a Kenny Rand here?" I COULDN'T BELIEVE IT. He was calling out my name. Some consider Mays to be the greatest baseball player of all time, and here he is, calling my name.

After the shock wore off, I shouted, "It's me, it's me". Willie then said (I now know him on a first-name basis), "Happy Birthday, Kenny; I think you have something for me to sign." My shaking hands somehow gave him the ball, and then he signed it and smiled at me. I looked at the ball, which said, "Happy Birthday, Kenny," and it was signed in the classic, yet almost unreadable, signature, "Willie Mays."

The great Willie Mays (1958).

May's unreadable signature.

I thanked him and asked him if he could hit a home run for my birthday. He just smiled at me and continued signing autographs for other kids. King of the World does not describe how I felt. The very common text message of today's generation, which says "OMG, OMG, OMG," would have been appropriate at that time. I can still feel the stares and envy of the other kids screaming for his autograph.

I returned to my seat beside my dad, wondering how I could even begin to express my gratitude. I know I must have said, "Thanks, Dad?" but I was more curious about how my dad could arrange this miracle. I looked at him with the bewilderment that only a 12-year-old can have, and before I asked him, he told me that Uncle Jack had helped to arrange it.

Think about it: box seats at a Giant game in Philadelphia, meeting Willie Mays, and getting a personalized autograph... what a birthday gift. By the way, Willie Mays did hit a home run that night and threw out a runner at home plate. I recall that the Giants won 4 to 1, but who cares? I wish I still had the ball to authenticate this fantastic story. However, if you read the recent autobiography of Willie Mays, you will find verification of this story. The top photo is the great Willie Mays, the photo below is not the ball that he signed that day, which was probably lost when we moved, but it does show his almost illegible signature.

CHAPTER NINE

Television, Music and Movies (1955 – 1958)

- **Television**

After we moved to Walden Terrace, our parents bought a new television. Now, instead of having just one TV set we have two. And there were three national TV companies (NBC, ABC, and CBS), and three local stations. This increase in viewing options came at the right time because, as a family, we began to develop our own individual tastes.

Television programming was now moving into what has been called 'The Golden Age' of Television. There were still many shows that we enjoyed as a family such as *I Love Lucy* show, which was still the #1 sitcom in terms of popularity. There was also a TV game show hosted by Groucho Marx titled *You Bet Your Life,* and every family's favorite, the *Ed Sullivan* variety show.

Our parents didn't watch the *Walt Disney Disneyland* TV show, which debuted in 1955, but my siblings and I loved it. The Disney hour featured four different themes (Adventure Land, Frontierland, Tomorrowland, and Fantasy Land). My favorite was Frontierland, which ran a series on American folk hero, Davy Crockett, played by actor Fess Parker. This show was so popular that it even had a hit song, "The Ballad of Davy Crockett":

Born on a mountain top in Tennessee
Greenest state in the land of the free
Raised in the woods so's he knew every tree
Killed himself a bear when he was only three

One year later, Disney produced the iconic *Mickey Mouse Club*, an afternoon series featuring the 'Mouseketeers'. One of the Mouseketeers, Annette Funicello (see photo below), became an instant star and the crush of millions of teenage boys. This young star went on to marry the very popular singer, Eddie Fisher. Many of you probably know that this show was a starting point for numerous other entertainers, including Justin Timberlake, Britney Spears, and Christina Aguilera.

Annette Funicello (Age 14).

Another classic TV show from the early 50s was *The Adventures of Superman*, starring George Reeves as reporter Clark Kent and comic book hero Superman. This show aired from 1952 to 1957 and became a Saturday afternoon classic, helping to promote the "Superman" franchise, which includes comics and movies. The photo on the left shows George Reeves as Clark Kent, a reporter for the Daily Planet newspaper. On the right is Superman and his girlfriend, Lois Lane.

Clark Kent (aka Superman)   Superman and Lois Lane

My brother Frankie, also loved to watch the *Friday Night Fright* horror movies, which featured the original films of *Frankenstein* (1931, starring Boris Karloff *Dracula* (1931, starring Bela Lugosi), and *The Wolf Man* (1941, starring Lon Chaney). Although these movies were released many years before TV, they were relatively new to the television industry. Boo! This era saw some significant changes in TV programming, and by 1957, almost 90% of all American families had at least one television set.

- **Music:**

Tom & Jerry (Music Hall of Fame). In 1958, I was in JHS, and my brothers Frankie and Binnie were in the 10th and 11th grades of Forest Hills High School. One day, Binnie came home with a 45-rpm record that he had bought at a school concert. The record was by a high school singing duo named Tom and Jerry. In a few short years, Tom and Jerry changed their stage names to Simon and Garfunkel and went on to sell millions of records and albums.

They soon became two of the most iconic recording artists of their era. To this day, their song titled "Sound of Silence," is, in my estimation, is one of the best songs ever written.

Hello, darkness, my old friend
I've come to talk with you again
Because a vision softly creeping
Left its seeds while I was sleeping
And the vision that was planted in my brain
Still remains
Within the sound of silence

Music is slowly changing, and Rock 'n' Roll is beginning to take over the radio stations. Singer Fats Domino was at the top of the music charts with "Ain't That a Shame". The song "Sixteen Tons" by Tennessee Ernie Ford was also a huge hit.

Another popular song was "Love Is a Many Splendored Thing" by the Four Aces, which became one of the all-time great ballads. **"Rock 'n' roll" music** finally hit the charts with "Rock Around the Clock," by Bill Haley and His Comets. Other rock n roll songs from 1955-1957 that became classics were,

1955: "Tutti Frutti" by Little Richard, "Maybelline" by Chuck Berry, and the ballad, "Only You", by the Platters.

1956: "Hound Dog" and "Don't Be Cruel" by Elvis Presley and," Be – Bop- A - Lula" by Gene Vincent.

1957: "That'll Be the Day" - Buddy Holly, "Great Balls of Fire" by Jerry Lee Lewis. "Jailhouse Rock" and "All Shook Up" by Elvis Presley and "Diana" by Paul Anka. "Rock 'n' Roll" was now the popular choice of teenage music lovers and began to dominate most of the radio stations.

• **Elvis**

If Alan Freed was the king of radio, Elvis would soon become the King of Rock 'n' Roll. Born in Tupelo, Mississippi, local singing sensation Elvis Presley made his national TV debut on January 28,

1956, on the Dorsey Brothers Variety show. He appeared on this show for nine episodes, but Elvis became super famous after appearing on the national *Ed Sullivan TV Show.*

Mr. Sullivan was reluctant to invite Elvis to his show because he wanted to avoid the controversy that surrounded Elvis' appearances. However, on July 9, 1956, Elvis made his first appearance on the show.

Elvis shown from the waist up.

Elvis went on to do six more Sullivan shows and soon became an international recording star. Early in his career, Elvis experienced a lot of unfair press. Knowing this, Mr. Sullivan made it a point to say on live TV that Elvis "is a fine young man." In doing so, he was answering the negative controversy over Elvis's' fabricated reputation.

Elvis' first two hit songs, "That's Alright Mama", and "Hound Dog" were 'cover' songs previously recorded by Arthur 'Big Daddy' Crudup (1946) and Willie Mae 'Big Mama' Thornton (1952), respectively. Elvis's first movie, *Love Me Tender,* was titled after his hit song, and he went on to make 32 (that is a lot) more movies, all of them box office hits.

Elvis singing on the Dorsey Bros. TV show.

- **Teen Idols**

Elvis had a lot of company in terms of teenage idols. There were a number of young male singers and actors who became heart throbs of the young female public. Do you remember these good looking 'American Idols?'

Paul Anka
Fabian
Frankie Avalon
Tab Hunter
Ricky Nelson

- **Movies**

My siblings and I still loved going to the movie theater on the weekends. The movie, *Rebel Without a Cause*, was a huge box office hit featuring the charismatic, young and rising movie star James Dean, and the film, *The Seven Year Itch*, was popular and showcased actress Marilyn Monroe. It is said that this movie helped propel her to instant fame both as an actress and as a sex symbol. Marilyn was a model before she became an actress, and her photos in Playboy magazine also contributed to her international stardom.

Between Elvis's hips and Marilyn's curves, the two of them are probably responsible for starting the sexual revolution. Perhaps the age of innocence is not so innocent? Below is probably the most iconic of all Marilyn Monroe's poses. Summer is rapidly approaching, and new adventures await.

One of her most iconic photos.

CHAPTER TEN

Brown's Hotel (1954 - 58)

I must have been either 8 or 9 years old when my dad was offered the prestigious job as band leader at Brown's Hotel in Loch Sheldrake. Browns was just one of many resort hotels in the Catskills, but it ranked among the top three hotels in terms of reputation and size. The two other popular hotels were the Concord and Grossinger's. All three hotels had beautiful grounds, tennis courts, large indoor lobbies, and numerous swimming pools.

To help compete with these other two hotels, Brown's built a brand-new auditorium (theater) called the Jerry Lewis Playhouse. The world-famous comedian and actor Jerry Lewis had one of his first jobs as a waiter at a nearby hotel, also owned by the Brown's family.

The main building and beautifully landscaped front lawn.

Charles and Lillian Brown, due to high summertime demand, built adjacent buildings nearby. In the 1950s, the hotel's capacity was around 800 people. By 1960, after the newly attached wing with luxury rooms was completed, the hotel could then accommodate approximately 1,200 guests. On the right side of this photo was a covered walkway that led to the new Jerry Lewis Theater.

Just looking at the above photo instantly brings back a flood of memories and nostalgic feelings. In spite of the hotel's "luxury" status, the guest rooms in the main building were surprisingly small. How small, you ask? A Saturday night comedian who appeared at the hotel loved to tell the following joke: "I want to that the Brown family for allowing me to stay overnight. However, I don't want to say that my room was small, but when I put my key in the door, I broke the back window."

The kidney shaped pool with the newly luxury
suites Behind it on the right.

• Where We Stayed

During our first summer at Brown's, we stayed at a board-ing house (now known as a B&B), which was about three miles away. However, in the 2nd summer (1955), we stayed at Richman's Bungalow colony, which was located across the road from Brown's and was within walking distance. We stayed at Richman's for the next ten summers, until my dad was able to negotiate getting a room at the hotel.

Our bungalow was at the top of a hill, and the driveway to it was an old dirt road. The colony had about eight bungalows, of which ours was one of the largest, (we had six family members). My guess is that all the other bungalows were occupied by hotel employees.

Our bungalow. The 4th one on the left.

- **More About The Hotel**

Brown's Hotel had something for everyone. For young kids there was a day camp run by Murray and Bertha Shapiro. For teens, it featured a teen clubhouse, a teen pool, and a teen rock 'n' roll band. For adults, it had numerous daytime and evening activities. In fact, it was very similar to the cruise ships that are popular for today's travelers.

After breakfast, guests could play volleyball and basketball, go on field trips (such as horseback riding), or sit and relax by the pool. They could even partake in the entertaining exercise hour on the pool stage led by athletic director Sam Tolkoff. After lunch, there was a softball game, a diving exhibition, and swimming lessons led by diving expert Johnny Grant. Or guests could sit by the pool and listen to the live music of a Latin band or get free dance lessons from Johnny and Linda Renee.

A few hotel guests stayed for extended periods, but over 90% of the families stayed for one week. This is important because Sunday was the check-in and checkout day when most guests left the hotel to return home to their homes in New York City, Westchester, or Long Island. While they were leaving on Sunday, an equal number of new guests arrived for their one-week vacation. The photo below is part of Brown's brochure and has three pictures:

The cover of the Brown's Hotel brochure.
That's my brother Johnny sitting on the lounge.

• **Family Fun**

Our summer family activities were not limited to the hotel. My dad, in the summers, had a lot of free time and made sure that we took advantage of the beautiful surroundings of the Catskill Mountains. Dad also took us on frequent hikes to a nearby mountain called Mt. Baldy. Mom wasn't a fan of hiking, but my siblings and I loved it. Mt. Baldy was about 2,000 ft above sea level and it was a challenge to climb. The reward of seeing a view of the entire Catskill mountains was well worth it. Before we left on our trip, Dad packed us lunch, and when we arrived at the top, we ate our lunch while enjoying the incredible panoramic view. Going back down from the summit of Mt. Baldy was a lot easier than going up.

I also recall the time he took us to a famous tourist site called Howe's Caverns. The car ride took almost three hours, but the wait was well worth it. These caverns were located approximately 200 feet below ground level. Besides having underground caves with their stalactites (long icicles growing from the top of the cave) and stalagmites (which grow up from the ground), the caverns also had an underground river with a boat ride. I clearly remember getting the people in our boat to sing the then-popular "Ballad of Davy Crockett" song during our boat ride.

Then there was the unforgettable trip to Devil's Canyon near Niagara Falls. It is now known as Devil's Hole State Park and is a popular tourist destination. However, when we went there (1956), it was not well known and rarely visited. The trip to this canyon and falls produced another scary moment for me. Above the canyon, was a flat area of slate rock approximately 100 feet long and 100 feet wide. Flowing over the smooth rock slate was a steady stream of shallow water that led to a cliff and the falls.

At that time, there wasn't any guardrail for safety purposes. I don't know why I did this, but I walked over the wet slate and stood right at the edge of the cliff and watched as the magnificent falls dropped down about 200 feet. My body instantly froze. I couldn't move. It was so breathtaking. Somehow, I found the courage to slowly step back to safety. My dad, of course, was upset at me for taking this risk, and he was right. I now have an immense fear of heights (acrophobia) that seems to get worse as I get older. Another unadvised adventure awaits.

- **Shotgun Annie**

What a perfect name for a myth. Get ready for an adventure that should be in a movie. About 200 feet across the hotel was a two-lane highway (Route 52). If you walked across Route 52 for about 100 ft., there was a small lake owned by the hotel. It wasn't much of a tourist site, and to my knowledge, no guests ever used it for any reason. There wasn't any walkway from the highway to the lake, just a dirt path that would often be muddy if it had recently rained. A rowboat was available, but again, no one used it.

The lake had a legend. At the far end of the lake, there supposedly lived an old lady, nicknamed "Shotgun Annie". No one had ever seen her or had an encounter with her. So, she must be a myth. Right??

In the summer of 1957, my oldest brother, Frankie, decided that we should investigate whether the myth was fact or fiction. Frankie, Binnie, and I all got in the rowboat and bravely rowed to the opposite end of the lake. Throughout this short trip, we spent our time joking, laughing, and eating peanut butter and jelly sandwiches.

As we got closer and closer to the far side, our moods slowly began to shift in anticipation of what might happen. Suddenly, when we were only 50 feet from the shore, we saw shotgun pellets piercing the water near our boat. The myth is true. And there she was, about 100 feet away, looking right at us, aiming her shotgun to shoot again. She looked about 100 years old with wild gray hair, wearing dungarees, no shoes, and a plaid shirt and she was no taller than 5 feet. I couldn't believe what I was witnessing. We looked at each other, then instantly panicked, and jumped into the water. We quickly turned the boat around to protect ourselves and used our arms as oars to get as far away as possible. When we were about 200 feet away, hopefully out of shotgun range, we all jumped back into the rowboat. Frankie laughed and said, "Let's go back to the hotel", and we rowed, as fast as we could back to the hotel. The trip back was filled with an empty silence from the three of us.

What an experience. I know we told our dad, but he didn't believe us. He thought we made up the story. And so, the legend lives on.

- **"Drive!"**

It was a partly cloudy day; the light wind and the clouds kept the sun from being too hot. We were in Dad's 1956 Chevy, and he was driving us through some old country roads about ten miles from the hotel. The year is 1958 and I am twelve years old.

This was not the normal two-lane highway. The road had two lanes, but I don't believe it was wide enough for two cars to actually pass each other. And there wasn't any road line to separate the two lanes. I don't recall a single straight stretch of driving on this road.

It was all curves and hills, and the scenery of farms and land was a picturesque thirty shades of green. Every mile we drove, we could see cows grazing and chickens doing what chickens do. So many chickens.

Dad soon pulled over and stopped the car. I thought he wanted to just take in the scenery. I was wrong. He told us to get out. I was in the back seat with Binnie and Judy, while Frankie was in the front seat. Dad looked at me, handed me the keys, and said, "Drive. It's your turn." *What?*

I could hear my siblings jokingly say "NO, NO, don't let him." I looked at Dad and said, "Dad, I'm twelve years old, are you serious"? He just smiled and sat next to me in the passenger seat. I may be twelve, but I am a big twelve. I was now 5'9" and the tallest in the family.

I think everyone remembers the first time they ever drove a car, but that is usually in some supermarket or school parking lot. Not on a winding country road. There were many previous times when I was alone with dad in the car, sitting next to him, when he would let me take the steering wheel and help him drive, but this is different.

Anyway, who am I to not trust my wise dad? And I am not crazy enough to blow my first chance to actually drive a car. What ensued was a roller coaster country road ride of a lifetime. Hill, after hill, curve, after curve. I had driven bumper cars at an amusement park, but this was a different thrill altogether. I can sense that you are waiting for something bad to happen. Your instincts are good. Well, it was not really bad, but it was really scary.

The only instruction from dad was him saying, "Drive slow, don't go above 30 miles per hour". I was driving very well…until… in the distance, I saw a car approaching us coming from the other direction. I'm thinking, *OMG*. Dad said, "Kenny, just drive slow and you'll be OK". But something strange happened. When I lightly put my foot on the brake to slow down, the car started speeding up and went faster. *OMG*. The more I tried to slow down the faster we went. He's getting closer. *OMG*. My siblings were screaming and holding on for dear life. Dad turned to them and shouted, "Shut up". By the time we passed by each other I was going about 60 miles per hour, though it felt like 100 miles per hour.

I obviously put my foot on the gas pedal and not the brake. Anyway, we lived. But I gave my family the ride of their life and I was simultaneously thinking that I may never drive again.

Here is a related true story. I was the best driver in my Driver Education class in high school. I know this because one day our instructor, after driving us around, pulled into a gas station in downtown Ardsley. He got out of the car and told the four of us who were in the car, "I need to pick up my car. Kenny is going to drive you back to the school". And he whispered in my ear, "I trust you. You're the best and leave the keys in the car." Wow, that was quite a compliment, and yes, I now know the difference between a gas pedal and the brake pedal although my wife will disagree.

• Johnny and Linda Renee

The hotel, among its many amenities, featured a professional dance team, Johnny and Linda Renee, who offered private dance lessons to hotel guests. Like the rest of the hotel staff, they excelled in their roles. Each morning, they would offer a 'free' dance lesson on the pool stage, where they would teach hotel guests one or two steps to a variety of Latin dances, such as the Cha-Cha, the Mambo, the Tango, and others.

The two of them enjoyed watching my brother, Binnie, and me dance, and they took us under their wings and gave us free ballroom dancing lessons. A few years later, they introduced both of us to the world of professional dancing.

One of my first dance partners at the hotel was a girl named Gail Brust, and I am fortunate enough to have saved the photo below, which shows the two of us dancing the Cha-Cha before the evening show.

Gail and I on the theater stage.
I am eleven years old.

• Entertainment in the Catskills

One of the reasons for the success of the Catskills was the combination of their hospitality, great food, and the incredible evening entertainment which hotel guests could enjoy for free. Yes…. FREE. It was all part of the package.

Current celebrities of that era appeared on Saturday evening shows, including Bob Hope, Frank Sinatra, Sammy Davis Jr., Steve Lawrence and Eydie Gorme, Billy Crystal, Jerry Lewis, Buddy Hackett, Joan Rivers, Rita Moreno, and many more. For those of you who do not recognize these names, trust me that these were some of the biggest and most popular acts in show business.

The Catskills were also the breeding ground for many comedians from all over the country. Most of them, who had originated their acts in New York City, brought their skills and refined them for the Jewish clientele of the Catskill Mountains. People like Sid Caesar, Mel Brooks, Jackie Mason, Rodney Dangerfield, Jerry Stiller, Red

Buttons, Henny Youngman, Phyllis Diller, Woody Allen, and the list goes on and on.

This was clearly "A Time Like No Other".

- **Jerry Lewis**

Jerry Lewis, in the late 1950s and 1960s, was one of the most popular entertainers in the United States, if not the world, and I have some great Jerry Lewis stories, but you will have to wait. The comedian Jerry Lewis, appropriately received the nickname "The King of Comedy." Not forgetting his comedic roots in the Catskills, he formed a strong bond with Charles and Lillian Brown.

For those of you who have never heard of Jerry Lewis, all I can say is that you missed out on someone very special. Mr. Lewis rose to fame in 1946 when he teamed up with crooner Dean Martin. Their breakup as a team in 1956 shocked the entertainment world. Their separation can probably be compared to the breakup of the Beatles.

As a solo artist, Jerry Lewis went on to make 29 more movies. He was a super-talent. He was an actor, director, musician, singer, dancer, and comedian. In 1956, he had a hit song, "Rock-a-bye Your Baby," which reached #10 on the Billboard hit chart. It is said that Jerry Lewis was much more appreciated by the French public than the American critics.

In 1966, Jerry Lewis may be best known for being the host of the MDA (Muscular Dystrophy Association Telethon. This Labor Day TV celebration was on the air for 21 consecutive hours featuring entertainers from all over the world. During the next 44 years, Jerry Lewis and his friends helped to raise almost 2 ½ billion dollars for 'his kids'.

Dean Martin, one of the great crooners, went on to have numerous hits, including "That's Amore", "Mambo Italiano", and who can forget, "Volare", and then there is," Everybody Loves Somebody Sometime." If I close my eyes, I can hear him singing one of his biggest hits.

Everybody loves somebody sometime
Everybody falls in love somehow
Something in your kiss just told me
My sometime is now

Dean Martin also went on to have a movie career, and he also had a weekly hit TV show featuring his singing talents and special guests.

The Browns were proud of their relationship with the world-famous comedian, and they built a nightclub theater to honor his legacy. In the theater, they had cartoon images of Jerry Lewis. Below is a photo of the mural inside the Jerry Lewis Theater. The photo on the right, (1950), shows Dean Martin and Jerry Lewis, often regarded as the greatest comedy team of all time. Dean Martin is on the left and Jerry Lewis is on the right.

The mural in the theater club.   Dean Martin & Jerry Lewis

In my opinion, there was another entertainer in this era who surpassed the talents of Jerry Lewis and that personality was Sammy Davis Jr. I was able to see him perform at the hotel and I was in total awe of this multi-talented performer. His singing was first class, and he also told jokes, danced, and played the drums, trumpet and the piano. Mr. Davis had some very good friends in Hollywood as was part of the famous "Rat Pack".

In the photo below, (left to right) is Frank Sinatra, Dean Martin, Sammy Davis Jr., Peter Lawford, and Joey Bishop.

Here are the lyrics to one of Sammy Davis's most popular songs.

I knew a man
"Bojangles" and
He'd dance for you
In worn out shoes
With silver hair
A ragged shirt
And baggy pants
He would do the old Soft Shoe

The summer of 1958 is now over. And, yes, once again, we would move. This move took us away from the hustle and bustle of New York City, into the tranquility of living in the suburbs (and no more gangs).

BREAKING NEWS (1955- 1958)

Did You Know that …

- **In 1955**, Dwight Eisenhower was still President.
- Disneyland opened in Anaheim.
- James Dean died in a car crash.
- The first McDonalds opened.
- **In 1956**, The Montgomery Boycott ended.
- Elvis's "Heartbreak Hotel" becomes a #1 hit.
- **In 1957,** Russia launched the first Sputnik satellite.
- **In 1958**, Elvis is inducted to the Army.
- Pizza Hut, and IHOP open their first stores.
- NASA is formed.
- The US population is 175 million and expectancy is 70 years.

Famous people born in this period:

- **1955:** Bruce Willis, Kevin Costner, Whoopi Goldberg
- **1956**: Tom Hanks, Carrie Fisher, Joe Montana
- **1957**: Gloria Estefan, Spike Lee, Melanie Griffith
- **1958:** Ellen DeGeneres, Angela Bassett, Madonna, Sharon Stone

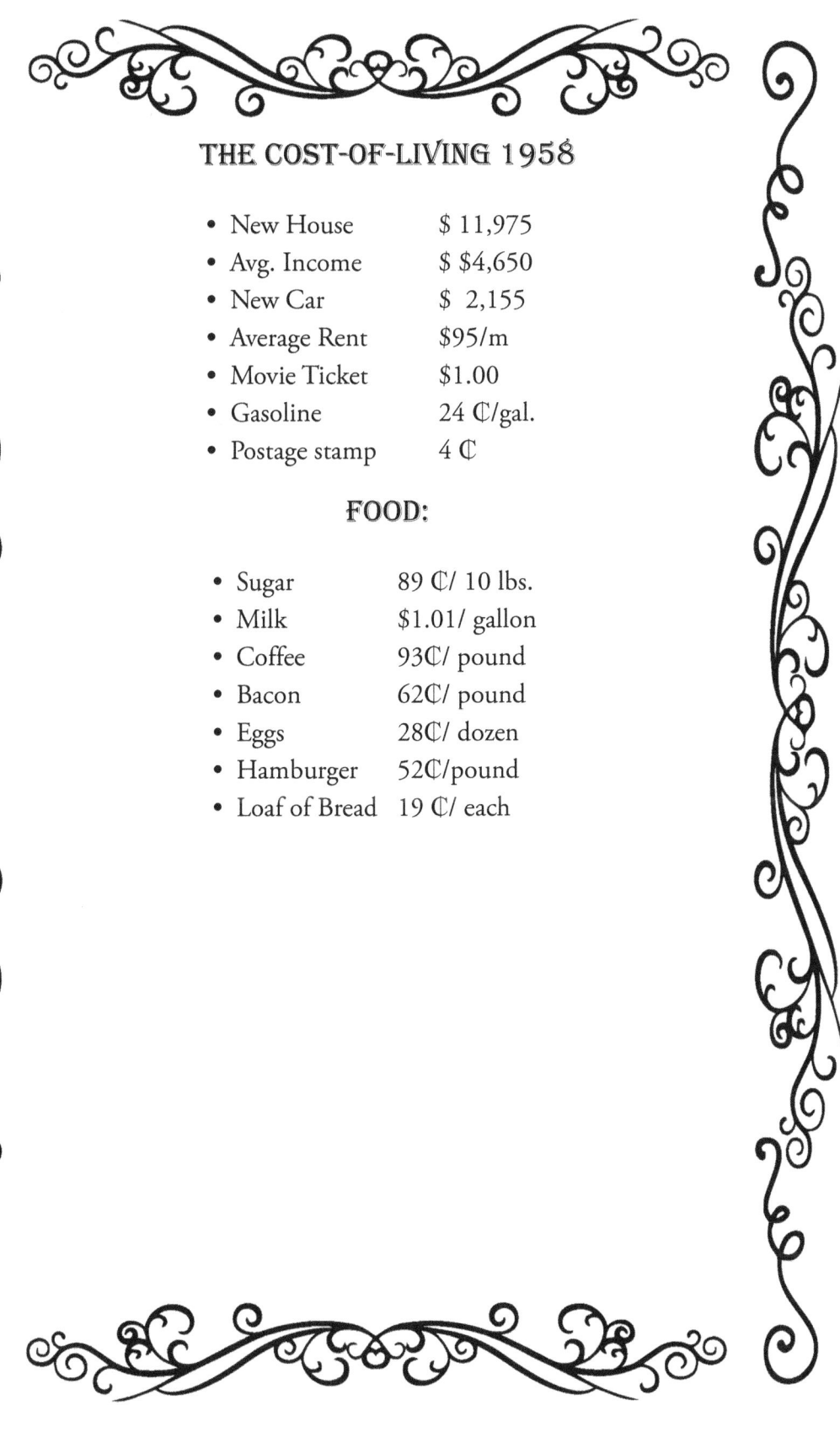

THE COST-OF-LIVING 1958

- New House $ 11,975
- Avg. Income $ $4,650
- New Car $ 2,155
- Average Rent $95/m
- Movie Ticket $1.00
- Gasoline   24 ₵/gal.
- Postage stamp   4 ₵

FOOD:

- Sugar   89 ₵/ 10 lbs.
- Milk $1.01/ gallon
- Coffee   93₵/ pound
- Bacon   62₵/ pound
- Eggs   28₵/ dozen
- Hamburger   52₵/pound
- Loaf of Bread   19 ₵/ each

FAMILY ALBUM

Mom's Family: Left to Right
Aunt Marie, Aunt
Junie, Uncle Bo,
Aunt Caty, Mom

Frankie (3), Me (6 months, Binnie (2)

Curly haired me
(six months)

Judy (4) and Me (5)

Bronx rooftop: Left to right:
Binnie, Frankie, and me, in
the back, are Dad and Judy

In Front: Judy (3), Me (4), In
the back Binnie (6), Frankie (7)

Left to Right: Cousin
Joanie, Judy, Me, Cousin
Kay, and Cousin Dabby

That's me with the curly hair in
the back row Johnny is in the
front row (left) 9 yrs. old

1950: Mom with
her mink stole

1961: Passover Dinner: Left to right:
Me Frankie, Dad, Johnny, Mom,
Uncle Jack, unknown, Judy

1995 Left to Right: Judy, Frankie,
Binnie Me, and Johnny

Mom & Dad in a tender moment

Part IV: 1958 - 1963

CHAPTER ELEVEN

Dobbs Ferry/Ardsley

The move to Westchester County was great timing. Leaving Forest Hills at the time we did, meant that I was going to live my life without the fear of getting stabbed and killed by a gang member. I was also thrilled that our family would finally have our own home rather than living in another apartment.

Before we moved, my parents would frequently take us on a ride to see our new home going through its stages leading to its completion. It was exciting to see our home go through the process during its construction and I can still smell the freshly cut wood that framed our home. Each trip brought us closer to the actual move in date.

A few weeks before the summer of 1958, our home was finished, and we finally moved into our new home in Dobbs Ferry in upstate New York. Dobbs Ferry, what an intriguing name for a town. It sounds like a fictional town from a novel about growing up in South.

Dobbs Ferry was a suburb of New York City. Even though it was relatively close to the city, a 30-minute drive, it was light-years away in terms of the scenery and culture compared to NYC. Our home was about three miles inland from downtown Dobbs Ferry which bordered on the Hudson River. The landscape was marked by beautiful rolling hills and tree-lined streets. And fresh air. Our backyard had huge pine trees, and the daily smell of the trees was refreshing and exhilarating.

I was 12 years old when we moved from Forest Hills, Queens, and to me, our brand-new home and the surrounding hills and trees in Dobbs Ferry were like living on a distant planet. Everything differed from the crowded and tall apartment buildings and the variety shades of gray buildings that helped to define the buildings in New York City.

Even though we had made many previous trips to the hotels in the Catskill Mountains of upstate NY, I never imagined that we would eventually live in an area that was so beautiful. Living in Dobbs Ferry, had the best of both worlds. It was close enough to New York City to still drive and visit, yet it was far enough away that its tranquility offered a more comfortable and different lifestyle.

My mom quickly made some changes to our new home and added a beautiful bay window overlooking our street (Northfield Ave). And she also went 'pink' crazy. Mom was a big fan of Marilyn Monroe, whose favorite color was pink. It wasn't long before Mom asked Binnie and me to paint the house a bright coral pink. It was so readily identifiable that we never shared our address with anyone. We almost embarrassingly said, "It's the pink house' and you can't miss it."

Dobbs Ferry was an upper middle-class town. Our home, which cost around $32,000 in 1958, was a lot higher in price than the national average of $12,000. This difference probably had to do with the fact that Dobbs Ferry was in a high-income area.

Our home had four floors. Under the beautiful bay window on the left side was huge basement (about 20 x 25 feet) that my mom had us turn into a den. Binnie and I tore out the back wall in the basement and installed another bay window, this one facing our backyard, which was about 100 feet away from the pine tree-lined Saw Mill River Parkway.

Binnie had early engineering skills. My skill was in passing him the hammer. The upper windows in the above photo were for two of the four upstairs smaller bedrooms. There were also two bathrooms, a master bedroom, and another smaller bedroom.

When my oldest brother, Frankie, moved out after graduating from high school, and using Binnie's skills, we broke down the wall between those two upstairs bedrooms and created an extensive master bedroom suite for our parents. The windows below the upstairs windows on the right side of the photo were garage windows. However, we never used it as a garage and turned it into a bedroom. Behind the front bay window, on the left side of the photo, was a large living room, a dining room, and a standard-sized kitchen that could accommodate a small dining table.

If you walked down our street for a few blocks, to the right of the above photo, you would find about 200 existing homes along Northfield Avenue that were probably built in the 1930s. On the left of the photo, there were ten more new homes on each side of the street. At the end of our street, there was a connecting street (Cyrus Field Road), which was a back road leading into the beautiful estates of Dobbs Ferry's rich and famous (J.D.Rockefeller, etc).

Dobbs Ferry and its neighboring town, Ardsley, were quintessential small-town America, with populations of approximately 4,000-5,000 people. The school district boundaries for Ardsley extended into the first few blocks of Dobbs Ferry, and my brothers, sister, and I were all enrolled in Ardsley High School. Ardsley was not a diverse community. In fact, I do not remember a single black or Hispanic family living in Ardsley.

Ardsley is somewhat famous for being the home of Mark Zuckerberg, who graduated from Ardsley High School many years after we had already moved from there. The gifted actor Pete Riegert, known for his roles in *Animal House* and *The Mask,* graduated one year after me. We weren't best friends, but we knew each other, and I remember attending the great swimming parties at his house.

In 1958, Ardsley, built a state-of-the-art High School, which was home for grades 7 – 12. Although the school had six grade levels, the total student population, while I was there, rarely exceeded 400.

Photo of Ardsley HS, taken in the fall of 2024.

It has now been over 60 years, and Ardsley High School still looks the same as it did when we moved there in 1958. The kids living on or near our street all went to Ardsley schools. The other High School, Dobbs Ferry HS, was in the heart of downtown Dobbs Ferry (about three miles away), and was our arch sports rival, and basketball was the focus of that rivalry.

There was only one main street in Ardsley, Heatherdell Road, that went through the middle of town. There were only a handful of stores in the downtown area, some of which were in a "V" Shape area near the Saw Mill River. It was what you would call 'a one-stoplight town'.

I recall that there was a drug store, a dry cleaner, a hardware store, a luncheonette (aka the 'Choc'), a small local grocery store (Riccio's), and a few others. The Saw Mill River, which itself was only about 15 – 20 feet wide, was about 20 feet away from the downtown businesses, and it was much more of a stream than a river (unless there was heavy rain, then it became a river).

Downtown Ardsley

My favorite store to shop at and the favorite of many families living in Ardsley, was the Riviera Bakery. Their fresh bread and unique cookies were 'to die for'. My personal favorites were the seven-layer chocolate cake, and the chocolate-covered cookie leaves that they usually saved for the holiday season.

Every time I travel from California to visit my brother in NY, my California teaching colleagues beg me to bring back some cookies from the Riviera Bakehouse. The problem is, I don't like to share. Just kidding.

I was saddened to find out that the bakery in Ardsley closed last year. Hoping to enjoy the same cookies and cakes at their sister bakery in Tarrytown, NY, It was also very disappointing when I visited their other store on my last visit, to find that they did not use the same baking style as the one in Ardsley. For those of us who frequent this bakery, a part of our history, other than the memories, is gone forever.

The Ardsley Riviera Bakehouse

CHAPTER TWELVE

8th and 9th Grade

- **Look Where You're Going**

I just recalled a funny incident (funny now, but not so funny then) that happened shortly after moving to Ardsley when I was in 8th grade. After playing basketball on the cement courts behind the old school, I got hungry and headed down to the local deli. As I was crossing the street, a car came upon me with three very cute teenage girls sitting in the front seat. I couldn't stop staring at them, and I could see them smiling and waving at me.

Well, I guess I stared way too long because the next thing I knew, I walked directly into a tree that was planted on the sidewalk next to the deli. BAM! OUCH! After my initial shock of pain and embarrassment, I quickly noticed that the girls in the car had broken into hysterical laughter. It was very embarrassing. That was a double whammy, both my face and my ego were bruised.

- **Another Lesson Learned**

I recall our first assembly at this new school in 1958. The student population was small enough for the new auditorium to accommodate all six grades (7–12). The reason I remember this assembly so well is that the program didn't start with the Pledge of Allegiance; it began with the Lord's Prayer.

Having only attended church on Christmas Eve and Easter Sundays (with my mom), I did not know the words to the Lord's Prayer. I felt incredibly embarrassed and stupid when the entire student population recited it. I know that my brothers also did not know the prayer and were equally embarrassed. My sister, Judy, who went to Catholic school when we lived in Forest Hills, was well versed in this prayer.

It is difficult to describe the discomfort of feeling so left out and ignorant. During my previous seven years of attending school in New York City, students were never asked to recite any prayer.

When we returned home, we informed our parents that we had been directed to recite the prayer. Both of our parents instantly became upset. Even though my mom was Catholic, she knew that religion had no place in public schools. The next day, my Jewish dad, with my mom's blessing, went to our school and vented his anger at the principal. He even threatened to sue the school, citing the Constitution, which, under the First Amendment, "prohibits the government (aka public schools) from establishing a religion or favoring one religion over another, ensuring religious freedom for all."

The principal ignored my dad, so my dad went to the local newspaper, which published and supported his request. Coincidentally, within a few weeks, articles appeared in The New York Times and other newspapers around the country about lawsuits being filed in New York to protect the separation of church and state. Evidently, Ardsley High School was not the only school in the state that was found to be violating the Constitution. When we had our next school assembly, the school administration, fearing lawsuits, no longer asked the students to recite the prayer.

I had no idea about the ramifications of my brothers and me being embarrassed and uncomfortable. Still, it was a valuable lesson in constitutional law and the reasons behind the separation of church and state. I am sure that the outcome angered some very religious people, but I also consider myself to be very religious, however, I do not believe that being religious should be an excuse for forcing or indoctrinating others to accept your religion.

A few years later, the Supreme Court ruled against public school prayers, and almost immediately, then-President John Kennedy, himself a Catholic, helped ease the tension by going on national TV to support the decision, citing that "We can all pray at our homes."

- **My First Kiss**

One of the benefits of having a younger sister was that she had many girlfriends. My sister Judy would often invite one, two, or even more of them to sleep over at our house for pajama parties. For a young male with hormones slowly taking over my life, this was like dying and going to heaven. One of her friends, Michele Pappas, was pretty and sweet. And as luck would have it, she also thought I was cute.

At 12 years old, I was way too young to go out on a date, so Michele and I would often go for walks and talk on the phone. Sometimes, we would walk along Ashford Avenue in Ardsley. This street was on the way to the old school, and directly across from the school was an old abandoned Victorian house. It must have been a beautiful home during its era, but it was now falling apart.

As Michele and I walked by this home, I asked her if she wanted to go inside and explore. She made a frown and said, "I heard that house was haunted". I laughed and said, "So what? It is so close to the street that if we scream, everyone can hear it." She laughed and reluctantly said, "OK". Michelle didn't know it at the time, but I had an ulterior motive. We carefully walked through the old three-story home, trying not to injure ourselves on the broken boards and floors. It was much darker inside the house than on the street, and I thought this would be the opportune time for me to steal a kiss.

This would not just be any kiss; it would be my first kiss. Michele quickly returned the favor. I thought I was going to faint right then and there. About a week later I bought her an ID bracelet, and we officially became a couple. Back then, it was very common for a boy to buy a girl an ID bracelet to signify the bond between them and let everyone else know that we were now a couple and were 'going steady'. I think it also had another message, which probably was a way of saying, 'hands off.'

Well, going steady with Michele did not last very long. After about two months, our eyes began to wander to the opposite sex more frequently than not. Our short romance was soon over. But Michele Pappas was my first-ever girlfriend, and I will never forget her.

- **Uncle (?) Jack and Johnny**

This is a short but necessary flashback. While we were living at Walden Terrace and before our move to Dobbs Ferry, our mom took a job at the prestigious Waldorf Astoria Hotel in New York City. While working there, she convinced the manager that they needed a place for their customers to store their briefcases, overcoats, and hats, and that she would be the perfect person to run this service.

Mom knew that the clientele at this hotel was wealthy, and they would most likely give her large tips to store their belongings and she was right. Each day, when she came home from work, she would ask us to help her count the dollar bills and quarters she had earned as tips. I suppose this was my early introduction to math. The significance of this side story is about to be revealed.

Uncle Jack

One day, after work at that hotel, Mom brought home a guest and introduced us to John Moon, who happened to live in Dobbs Ferry. Mr. Moon, wearing an expensive overcoat, looked rich and was rich. We later learned that he was a retired construction engineer and owned the company that helped build the Empire State Building and several other skyscrapers in downtown New York.

Mom told us that Mr. Moon was a frequent client at the Waldorf Astoria and that he wanted to meet our family. Mr. Moon, who came to our apartment about once a week, was not very tall, about 5'7", and he was a little on the chunky side. He had a large, round face and was very nice and friendly and carried a big smile. During his visits, he would often sit and talk or watch TV with us and occasionally stay for dinner. It wasn't long before all of us called him Uncle Jack.

I'm a young kid, but I'm not stupid. The thought that something might be going on between my mom and Uncle Jack was there, but my mind did not want to believe it, and it was never a prevalent thought in my daily life.

My Brother Johnny

In 1958, a few months before we moved to Dobbs Ferry, dad decided to legally change our family name from Temsky to Rand. He did this because of rampant antisemitism that was still left over from the McCarthy era. It is now over 60 years later, and rampant antisemitism still exists in our country today.

On September 29, 1958, my brother, Jonathan Arthur Rand, was born. Johnny's birth brought new life and enjoyment to our family. He was, and of course, still is, very lovable. He was a beautiful baby, always smiling at anyone who looked or played with him.

As Johnny grew up, he formed a close bond with me. When he was three years old, I was fifteen. Johnny and I spent countless hours wrestling with each other on the living room carpet, and occasionally, I would let him think he won to help boost his confidence. Even at this early age, he showed some athletic prowess. During the spring, I would take him out to the front yard and teach him how to catch and throw and hit a soft baseball. By the age of four, he was hitting a Whiffle ball like a seasoned professional. In the winter, we would spend hours on that lawn catching and throwing a football to each other.

I was in high school at this time, and each day I couldn't wait until I got home so that Johnny and I could have some fun, either playing ball, wrestling, or just watching TV. By the time he was eight years old, he was ready for Little League baseball and flag football. Again, wanting to spend time with him, I became his coach for both baseball and football. Here are some "Johnny" stories.

- **Flag Football Story**

Though these stories are out of chronological order, I hope you understand that this chapter may be the best place to tell them. The year was 1969, and Johnny was eleven years old. Johnny was the quarterback and also the defensive middle-linebacker on my flag football team. Once again, by the end of the season, our team was good enough to play in the championship game.

Both teams had identical records of 9 wins and 1 loss, and the opposing team had the best athlete in the league, whose name was Danny Abramowicz.

Let me set the scene. It was the fourth quarter; we were winning 12 – 7 in a tightly fought game. The game was almost over with only about 30 seconds to go. The other team, led by Danny, quickly advanced the ball down the field.

In the next play, Danny completed a pass to the seven-yard line, and there were now only five seconds left in the game and time for just one more play.

Danny went back to pass but couldn't find anyone open, so he tucked the football under his arm and started to run for the winning touchdown. Then, suddenly, from out of nowhere, Johnny ran across the field and 'tackled' him on the one-yard line. You need to remember that this was 'flag' football, not 'tackle' football. The game is over. but the arguments and controversy were not.

In professional football, a game cannot end with a defensive penalty. Although the flag football referees penalized our team by moving the football to the ½ yard line, the professional rule did not apply to our local flag football rules, and we still won the game.

That evening, I received about a dozen calls complaining that Johnny had broken the rules. However, to me, what Johnny did was nothing short of brilliant. His illegal tackle helped to make us win the Championship.

As we both got older, Johnny and I began to slowly drift apart. He was now in high school, and I was a teacher and living in my own apartment. Looking back, I feel that it was only natural for us to start living our own lives. This doesn't mean that we never spent time together, because we did. On many occasions, we would go shopping together, or I would come home for the weekend and watch him play baseball or football in his High School games.

Johnny was not only athletic, but he was also super good-looking. Speaking of shopping (and good looks), I have a cute side story to tell:

- **Shopping with Johnny**

One Saturday (Johnny was about 17 years old), Johnny and I went together to the Cross-County shopping center in Yonkers, NY. It was an outdoor mall with approximately 50 stores, and it was a beautiful spring day. We were hungry, so we decided to stop at a fast-food store to get some lunch.

As we walked in, I noticed about seven young ladies were working behind the counter. As soon as they saw Johnny, all seven jaws dropped simultaneously as if they had just seen Brad Pitt. I asked Johnny, "Did you see that?" Johnny just smiled. If I hadn't witnessed it, I wouldn't have believed it.

A few minutes later, we were outside the store eating our sandwiches, and an attractive young lady walked up to Johnny and asked him for the time. The weird thing was that we were standing under a rather large clock, which you could only miss if your eyes were closed. This time, Johnny and I exchanged laughs and big smiles.

My brother Johnny has it all. He is smart, athletic, and good-looking, but more importantly, he has a great personality and easily makes friends. He loves his family and is loyal to those who loved him. He is also mentally strong, which he needed when he suffered through some unfortunate tragedies and setbacks later in his life. I could not be prouder of my brother.

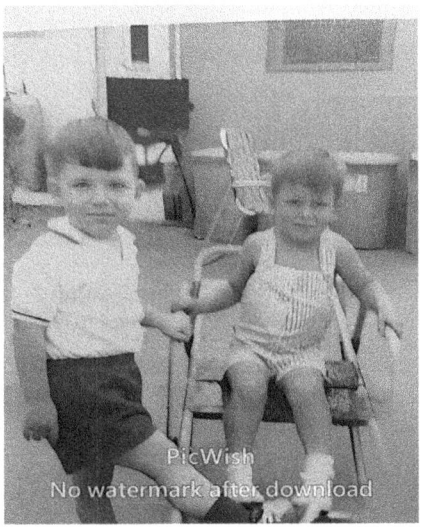
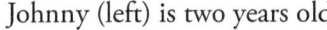

Johnny (left) is two years old	Johnny at 21. A photo from His modeling portfolio

Eat your hearts out, ladies. I told you he was good-looking (and he is also happily married).

• Back to Uncle Jack

A family secret is soon to be revealed. Everything is soon going to make sense.

About ten years ago, I received an angry phone call from Johnny. The call took me by surprise for two reasons. First, Johnny had never previously shown any anger directed at me. Never. Secondly, at the time of that call, I was in Las Vegas for a short vacation with my family, and we were having a great time; this call seemed to come out of the blue.

Johnny got right to the point and immediately asked me why I didn't tell him that Uncle Jack was indeed his father. To say his question threw me off guard is an understatement. I told Johnny the truth, which was that when he was born, I probably suspected that Jack might be his dad, but this speculation had lasted for only a fleeting moment. It just wasn't something that I ever dwelt upon. My siblings and I never discussed this possibility with each other, not once.

Maybe we were all in denial, but the fact is that it didn't matter to me. I was twelve years old when Johnny was born. I was interested in sports, girls, and loving my baby brother.

I can totally understand the anger that Johnny expressed on this phone call, but I was also confused. Uncle Jack never treated Johnny like a son, at least not in my eyes, and I am sure Uncle Jack did this to respect and maintain our family dynamics. Did my dad know? Well, either he was naive, in denial, or didn't care. To my knowledge, it was never discussed between my mom and dad or with the rest of the family.

My dad loved Johnny, period. He and Mom brought him up with the same love, discipline, and values that they did for all of us. I accept that Johnny is Jack's son. But it is difficult for me to pass judgment on my mom or dad. He was loved by both. It is also difficult for me to use the word 'half-brother'. It just doesn't sound right to me. It is not denial. Johnny is not half of being a brother. He is my brother.

Throughout high school I have had many great teachers and I will share them with you in a later story. However, not all the teachers cared about making a connection with their students.

- **My Sister Judy vs. Mr. Hester**

Mr. Hester had my sister Judy in his science class (1958-59). Hester was physically intimidating, standing at 6'4", and he had a stern and rigid Eastern European looking face and an army style crew cut. When Judy legitimately received a score of 100% on her final exam, he accused her (without any evidence) of cheating.

The next day, my dad accompanied my sister to the principal's office and requested an apology from Mr. Hester. The principal, unsure what to do, asked my dad if my sister would be willing to retake the test. My dad told him that my sister should not need to retake the test, and he was visibly upset. Judy turned to my dad and told him that she would be willing to retake the test right there in the office. She looked Mr. Hester in the eye and said, "I didn't cheat, and I want to prove it."

My dad reluctantly said, "OK". But he was still angry. Well, Judy took a similar test and finished it in about 20 minutes. Hester graded it right there in front of the principal, and once again, Judy got 100%. Hester gave my dad a weak apology. At which my dad said, "It's not me you owe an apology to. It's my daughter." Which Hester humbly did. Like you, I was wondering about the source of Hester's decision.

- **My Brother Frankie vs. Mr. Hester**

This is now 1959. My older brother Frankie was an excellent baseball player. Unfortunately, Hester was also the varsity baseball coach. When it was Frankie's turn to take batting practice during the tryouts, Hester, who was pitching, hit my brother with a fastball three times in a row.

It was evident to Frankie that this was intentional. Frankie was angry and, knowing he could not start a fight with a teacher, he physically and facetiously moved the home plate towards where Hester had thrown the three previous pitches. This gesture by Frankie sent Hester into a rage, and he told my brother to leave the field. Again, I wonder, *what does this have against my family?* There's more. In a later chapter where you will learn about my personal history with Mr. Hester.

- **Frankie's Graduation**

Sorry for the diversion. I hope you are ready to laugh out loud. I was in 9th grade (1959) when my oldest brother, Frankie, graduated from high school. Frankie had a terrible time in high school. By the time he was a senior, A very handsome Frankie had gained a lot of weight and was socially awkward. He hated school, and my memory tells me that he barely passed enough classes to graduate. Frankie was very bright but didn't apply himself.

Our entire family went to his graduation ceremony, and the auditorium was packed. The ceremony began without incident until something unusual happened. As the teachers and administrators were giving out awards to the graduates, we could hear a snicker of laughter coming from the graduates seated in the back rows of the benches on the stage.

My brother Frankie was sitting in the top row, where most of the noise was coming from. Suddenly, someone in his row farted, and every student in that row laughed so hard that they bent over in hysterics, holding onto each other as their seats began to shake. Not a good idea. The entire top row suddenly disappeared from view as all the students fell backward to the floor in laughter. I am still laughing while I am writing, as I can visualize this hilarious inopportune picture in my mind. The good news is that no one was hurt, and after hundreds of parents let out a roaring laugh, the ceremony was able to continue as if nothing had happened.

CHAPTER THIRTEEN

My Sophomore Year

- **The Rumble**

It all started on a Friday evening in my sophomore year (1960). I was at a HS dance party in the school cafeteria and about one hour into the dance party, many of us who were dancing on the cafeteria floor heard a commotion outside in the hallway that was near the exit doors right next to the cafeteria.

Suddenly, everyone (approximately 150 students) rushed to the area where the noise was coming from. When we arrived, we witnessed a heated argument between some of our HS seniors and potential intruders who were trying to crash into the dance party.

Within minutes, a few chaperone teachers came over, and they were able to disperse the potential intruders. The next day, I was playing in a pickup basketball game in the schoolyard behind the old school. As we were playing, one of our senior class friends drove up in his car and said that the kids from Yonkers (last night's intruders) had come here to pick a fight.

This did not sit too well with most of the older students, and they seemed to be instantly ready for anything. Within minutes, about four cars filled with students, including those of us at the basketball court, drove to where a possible fight might happen. In downtown Ardsley, across the street from the Riviera Bakery, was a small strip mall which had a drugstore, a supermarket, and a soda shop. My school friends quickly went into the soda shop to tell the kids from Yonkers to go home.

I'm not stupid, so I did not go inside. I quickly went over and leaned near a car about 15 feet away thinking that I was a safe distance from any possible action. Once everyone had left the store, the fight began. As I was getting ready to move even further away, a giant of a kid (6'4", 250 pounds) came over to me, picked me up, threw me about 10 feet away, and kicked me in my ribs. OUCH!! *What did I do?* I was just peacefully leaning on a car. I guess it was at the wrong place at the wrong time.

Within minutes, the town police came (all two of them) and took us to the city hall. Though I was in extreme pain, I was asked to go with them as a possible witness. After one hour, the judge sent everyone home with a warning, except for me. I went to the hospital and found out that I had two broken ribs. I'm a lover, not a fighter. Lesson learned.

- **My Favorite HS Teachers**

Not every high school teacher left an impression on me, but one who did was our 9th-grade home room and social studies teacher, Mr. Serniak. He was young, probably in his late twenties, and it was clear that he had a passion for teaching.

Mr. Serniak had a way of communicating that made learning enjoyable, and each day I looked forward to attending his class. This is one of the reasons that his unexpected death was so tragic and heartbreaking. It was a Monday in the Spring of '59, and we were sitting in his class, when a substitute teacher arrived. We were somewhat anxious because we heard rumors that he was in boating accident.

Within minutes, an announcement was made over the school PA system asking for a moment of silence in memory of Mr. Serniak. *What happened?* We all sat in a state of shock. It appears that he went on a weekend vacation with his wife and son to a lake resort in upstate New York. We were later informed that his son had fallen from the boat into the lake, and Mr. Serniak dove in to save him.

Unfortunately, the frantic movements of his son prevented him from getting a firm hold, and they both drowned. This tragedy was hard to process, not just for me but for anyone who knew him or had him as a teacher. Throughout my school years in New York City, I never experienced a school tragedy like this one.

There was another teacher at AHS (Ardsley High School) who made a great impression on me and strongly influenced my growth. My ninth-grade Algebra teacher, **Mr. Einhorn**, was excellent. Again, he was the type of teacher who made learning fun, and he was approachable, always smiling, and had a great sense of humor. He seemed to have a way of helping students build up their confidence, which, to me, is one of the key factors of 'learning'.

Mr. Einhorn made St. Patrick's Day a special event by always wearing green shoes and a green bow tie. He was way ahead of his time. His son, Steven, also happened to be in this Algebra class, and he, like his dad, had that positive outlook and enjoyed life. I had other great teachers, and I will tell their stories in the appropriate chapter.

The 'Choc': Our Hangout

Almost every day after school, students from our high school would go down (and I literally mean 'down') to the local luncheonette called the Chocolateria. Downtown Ardsley, where the 'Choc' was located, was a two-mile downhill walk from the High School. Quite often, when we went to the 'Choc', we would have an ice cream soda or milkshake, a snack, partake in some small talk, and listen to music on the jukebox.

This place was our daily hangout. No one called our hangout by its rightful name; we just called it the "Choc". The Choc had a serving counter with high stools and a few dining tables in the front room opposite the serving counter and the floor was the typical black and white square tiles. There was also a back room with a wide-open space leading into it, and it had more tables, a jukebox, and a bowling machine with automatic pins and a metal puck to try and knock them down. I usually lost this game while playing against my friends Carl and Creighton.

The owner of the Choc, Frank Pastore, was a retired postman and one of the nicest, most caring, and gentlest people you would ever meet. He loved kids, and he threw a weekly party there every Friday night. It was his way of giving back to the community and helping to keep us off the streets.

Because the Choc could not accommodate that many students (as the school population grew), my memory tells me that the weekly party was only for juniors and seniors, almost as if it were a rite of passage. Anyway, I think I fell in love with a different classmate at each party. The West Coast teens had their drive through soda and hamburger hangouts and we had our 'Choc'.

These were amazing times to be a teenager. Dancing to songs like "Mashed Potato Time" by Dee Dee Sharp, "Johnny Angel" by Shelly Fabres, "All I Have To Do is Dream" by the Everly Brothers, "He's So Fine" by The Chiffons, "So Much in Love" by The Tymes, and so many more. These songs are permanently ingrained in the memories of anyone living in this era.

Though the Choc is no longer there, the picture below shows where it used to be. (It's the store with the green awning). In my senior year, Frank sold 'The Choc,' which temporarily ended our Friday night parties. However, his love for kids prevailed, and he made a deal with the local school district by negotiating with them to open the cafeteria of the 'old' school for our parties.

The store with the green awning was our 'Choc'.

- **The Fonz:**

This is kind of surreal. Ardsley had its own 'Fonz'. His name was Denny Fonzarella. He attended Ardsley HS for a few years but dropped out a year before we moved there. His stories about getting in trouble with the law were legendary, almost as if he were a mythical character.

His nickname was, of course, The 'Fonz'. He was very short, about 5'5" tall, had wavy black hair, and yes, he wore a black leather jacket and drove a motorcycle. When we moved there, he was about 20 years old. I never met him, but I had a close encounter at a Friday night party at the home of one of my classmates.

About an hour into the party, whispers ran through everyone in attendance, "The Fonz is here." We all stopped what we were doing, hoping to get a glance at the legend. And suddenly, there he was, walking into the backyard in his Fonz clothes (jeans and black leather jacket). I have to admit that he was charismatic. I got only a short glimpse of him, but I could tell that he was not someone to mess with.

What is interesting is that many years later (1974), the TV show *Happy Days*, became a hit, featuring Henry Winkler as 'The Fonz' (Arthur Fonzarelli), whose style and character is a clone of Ardsley's own and original 'Fonz'.

• Another Choice

It was near the end of the school year when my dad sat me down and we had a father-son talk, and it wasn't about birds and bees. While we were home doing some chores together, he asked me to sit down next to him, and out of the blue he said, "Kenny, I want to talk to you about choosing a religion".

He told me that it was my choice, but he felt that it was import-ant to choose because having a religion gave someone a sense of 'belonging'. He also shared with me that both of my brothers chose to be Jewish, and my sister chose to be Catholic.

I didn't have to think about this. I instantly told him that I would not choose. He, of course, asked "Why?" I wasn't rude to him, it's just that I had already decided my thoughts. I told him that religion, which, among its many purposes, had the goal of bringing families together, but as happened in his own family, it also has the capacity to tear families apart.

I was, even at that young age, aware of the tensions between Israel and the Arab countries, which was a result of their different religious beliefs. To me this was just another example of how religion separated people.

Dad said, "You could choose to be a Catholic like your sister". I said, "Dad, there is too much hypocrisy in most religions. I have friends who go to Church every Sunday and then they use the "N" word on Monday". Dad said he understood, but he went on to tell me that religion, at its best, fosters community connections, and it serves as a source of belief beyond oneself. He finished by telling me that he hoped that one day I would change my mind. We never discussed it again.

My beliefs have not changed. I know in my soul that I am a very religious person. This is a great time to tell you more about our mom and Dad.

- **More About Dad.**

Our dad was a workaholic. By 1958, dad was in high demand for piano lessons. Every morning in would leave the house at 8:00 AM and he wouldn't arrive home until 10 or 11 PM. His reputation had reached a level where he was able to charge $50 for a 30-minute lesson (that was a lot of money in 1958).

For the next two years his daily driving route had him giving lessons throughout the five boroughs and Long Island. You can imagine that he came home exhausted. By 1960 he was able to rearrange his lessons so that each day all of his lessons were in the same borough.

No matter how tired he was when he came home, he was always there to help me study for a test or finish my book reports. He was never cranky or angry. He loved helping me and the rest of us. During the weekend is when dad made most of his income.

For example, on a Friday night he was usually asked to play at some musical event, then on Saturdays, he would play at a bar mitzvah in the afternoon and then a wedding in the evening. And he also had one or two gigs to play on Sunday. I remember helping him lift his new portable piano/organ into the back of his station wagon.

Dad was rarely home, but when he was home, he was a very loving father to all of us. Dad was rarely home even on special holidays like Thanksgiving, Christmas and New Year's Eve. These weekend jobs paid quite well, and he had a large family to feed.

I recall a time, when my siblings and I decided together that dad should at least spend one New Year's Eve at home with his family. We were all working at the time, and we each saved up $250, for a total of $1000 to give to dad as a birthday gift (November 21st) with the condition that he take off on New Year's Eve and not work.

When he opened his birthday card and saw the money and our plea with him to stay home, he got teary-eyed. He looked at us, then gave us back our money and said, "Thank you. I understand. You all worked hard for your money. I don't need it, and I promise not to work this New Year's Eve". This was a touching family moment, and I remember my mom crying and hugging everyone. Dad kept his promise.

Dad had an incredible 'dry' sense of humor and the older he got, the funnier he became. So many stories to tell and I will tell you just one for now (there are more great stories about Mom and Dad on my website, KenRand.net).

Dad would often have to carry heavy equipment to his performances (amplifier, organ, etc.) and he developed a torn hernia. While he was in the hospital to get it repaired, his nurse frequently asked him for some urine samples. One time, dad took the full cup containing the urine sample and emptied it in the bathroom sink and then he filled the empty cup with apple juice.

When the nurse came back, she asked for the urine sample and dad said, "Excuse me. Give me a minute. I am very thirsty". And then he took the cup and drank the apple juice. What was funny was the expression on the nurse's face. She thought that he drank the urine sample.

This photo shows dad sleeping after a hard day at work.

Truth be told, this photo was taken at Brown's hotel where he only worked three hours a day. LOL.

• **More About Mom**

We had two moms depending on if she was sober or had been drinking. It was very unpredictable; the only certainty was that she would be drinking on any given day. Our sober mom was very loving and caring and very affectionate. She had a great smile and an equally great personality with the uncanny ability to make friends, even with strangers. She was young enough to maintain her beautiful Irish red hair, though she spent way too many hours at the beauty parlor.

I remember this because I was the one to drive her there and pick her up when she finished. Mom never learned how to drive a car, nor did she ever learn how to swim. Anyway, to mom, the beauty parlor was a social gathering, and she made quite a few close friends there.

Mom's hobby was "shopping". I put that in quotes, but I should have typed, "SHOPPING" with all caps. And mom also had expensive tastes. I remember coming home one day from school when the entire living room looked different. There were new curtains, all new furniture, and a new carpet. I had to walk outside and check the color of the house to make sure I was in the correct place. No wonder dad had to work so much.

Mom made sure that the holidays were special. Again, she always invited her entire family to come to our home for Christmas dinner and of course there was the excitement of opening more gifts. So many great memories.

Sadly, I remember one Christmas, I think I was about 15 or 16 years old when things did not go so well. I was downstairs in the den with my siblings and cousins when I suddenly heard a lot of shouting going on. Within minutes, our aunts told my cousins that they were leaving. Apparently, mom had too much to drink and insulted one of her sisters.

I remember immediately feeling very awkward and lost. I was sad. I didn't know what to do. My brothers and I convinced mom to go upstairs and lie down, and we ended up doing all the dishes and cleaning up the dining room and the kitchen. None of us said anything to each other. There it is again. That terrible family dynamic of 'not sharing' our feelings with each other.

I recall so many times when I wanted to invite my friends over to the house after school, but I was afraid that she might have been drinking. It was not worth the risk. Then there were the times that mom asked me to drive her to a friend's wedding where it was an excuse for her to drink. She never got drunk at these weddings, but she drank enough to make me feel uncomfortable.

At home, Mom had different levels of drinking from just being tipsy to an all-out drunken stupor. Again, it was unpredictable and a nightmare for a teenage kid. I remember crying in my heart and saying, "Dad, where are you?" Of course, dad was working.

The following is a quote from a medical resource.

"Alcoholism, or Alcohol Use Disorder (AUD), is considered a chronic disease because it causes lasting,, harmful changes to brain structure and function, leading to a compulsive need to drink despite severe negative consequences. Recognized by major medical organizations like the American Medical Association and the American Psychiatric Association, it acts similarly to other chronic illnesses (like diabetes or heart disease) by requiring long-term management and impacting physical health, behavior, and decision-making."

Who am I to argue with medical science?

My alcoholic mom is not the mom I choose to remember. How can I be angry at someone who had a disease. That doesn't make sense. I have learned, other than sharing this because of my desire to be candid, to let go of that past. In my heart, I choose to remember mom as her best self, which is as good as it gets. We are all perfectly imperfect.

My beautiful Mom wearing her precious mink stole.
St. Mary's Park, Bronx, NY (1950)

CHAPTER FOURTEEN

Junior Year at AHS

- **My Closest Friends**

I am not sure that I would have survived the emotions I had from mom being an alcoholic, without having some close friends. Not that I shared my feelings with them, but our friendships created a distraction that allowed me to leave those feelings at home.

My closest friends in High School were Creighton Rayburn, Carl 'The tree' Meuser (he was 6'5"), Tommy Oliver, and Dave Reed. We hung out together throughout high school, and our bond grew even stronger in our senior year. I hope you enjoy the following stories about my friends and me.

In the yearbook photo above, in the front row (left to right) are Bobby Shields (a friend but not part of our clique), Creighton Rayburn, and me. In the back row (left to right) are Dave Reed and Tommy Oliver. It remains a mystery to me why our friend Carl was not in this photo.

I think Dave Reed was the only one in our group who had a steady girlfriend (Pam Patterson). The rest of us would usually hang out platonically with girls as friends. One night, we would go to Gail Rinciari's house, and the next night to Reggie Carlyle's home, or we would visit JoAnne Esposito's house.

I also had several female friends in lower grades with whom I became very close. I spent a considerable amount of time (hours) talking with Laurie Klein (my crush), and my friends Carolyn Ramin, and Shelly Flanders. I was still living at home when I was at college, and Carolyn and I kept in frequent touch; she even invited me to her senior prom..

Carolyn and me at her Prom.

• Peanut...Peanut Butter

The date is June 26, 1959. My friend Creighton invited Tommy and me, along with Dave, over to his house to watch the heavyweight championship fight between current champion Floyd Patterson and the Swedish champion Ingemar Johansson. While we were waiting for the battle to begin, all four of us got the munchies and Creighton obliged by making some peanut butter sandwiches, but unfortunately, he did not have any jam. Peanut Butter was and still is one of my favorite sandwiches, and I had it practically every day when I was in my teens, but I always ate it with strawberry or grape jam.

I'm not sure if you have ever had peanut butter without anything on it, but the taste and texture are very different. The following is a reenactment of our conversation while we were trying to eat our very dry sandwiches at Creighton's home.

Creighton: "Kennnnyyy, whyyyy are uuuu macking dose swilly faacces?"

Me: (I started to laugh) "Thhhisss peanut butttter isss getttinngg tuck inn mey mouse"

Creighton started to laugh. Then Tommy said: "Wazzz diz uuu saze?"

And then all four of us started laughing hysterically. The more we tried to communicate with each other, the more we laughed. Within minutes, all four of us were lying on the carpet laughing so much that my sides were hurting. Even just looking at each other with a smirk sent the four of us off into another round of hysterics.

Each time that one of us was foolish enough to try to talk, we would again burst into uncontrollable laughter. We must have set the Guinness record for the most extended continuous period of laughter without stopping. Oh my God. It was so funny. It was definitely a scene that would have sent the audience in a movie theater into tear-jerking laughter.

For the record, and to our disappointment, Johansson knocked out Patterson in the third round to become the new Heavyweight Champion. A few years later, at a packed Yankee Stadium (I was there with my family), Patterson, who had been the youngest fighter to win the coveted belt, returned the favor and became the first heavyweight fighter ever to regain the championship.

In their second fight, Patterson hit Johansson in the fifth round with a vicious left hook that knocked him out cold. How cold. Cold enough that Johansson's foot was shaking on the mat for a full five minutes after the knockout. An interesting side story happened when my family had a close encounter of the third kind with Floyd Patterson and his family, when we had dinner with them at their magnificent home in Scarsdale, New York.

Are you curious? My dad gave piano lessons to the children of Julius November, who was Floyd Patterson's financial advisor. The dinner and tickets to the fight were a favor that Mr. November gave to my dad. Below is the autographed picture from that evening.

Just a few weeks ago, I coincidently found this photo tucked away in some obscure drawer in my garage. The inscription says, "To Kenny, Best of luck, Floyd Patterson."

- **Making Another Choice**

This is not easy to write about, but it is an important part of my life.

It's Saturday, February 14th, 1961, and I am fifteen years old. For the past few months, I have been feeling more and more depressed. Maybe it was the winter blues? I am not sure why or if there was any one incident that precipitated this overwhelming feeling. Perhaps it was the effect of years ofo painfully listening to my parents argue. It's not that I am 'sad'. It is more of a sense of lacking self-worth. I felt flawed and believed that there was something wrong with me. This is not the first time I have felt this way. This has been going on my entire life. I was getting tired of feeling 'lost'. I don't think I ever felt so alone.

During this bout of depression, I read about a young teen who committed suicide by swallowing forty aspirins. I didn't have a gun, and stabbing myself or running in front of a speeding car were not the choices that I considered. So, on the date mentioned above, I decided to take 40 aspirins and end my life. Obviously, that did not work.

All that happened was that I got sick, and my parents had to rush me to the nearest hospital where they pumped out my stomach. The doctors and my parents soon knew the cause of my unexpected illness. I was sent home from the hospital, and I vividly remember that my dad was furious at me for trying to end my life. I remember his angry voice when he said, "How could you do this? Don't you know that you have a family that loves you. I think you are very selfish."

And he finished by saying, "And, if you ever try that again, I will kill you." He was trying to make a joke to ease the tension, and it worked. I immediately felt the love of my parents. Dad soon got more serious and asked the obvious question. "Why? Kenny what's wrong?" I am not a good enough writer to explain what I was going through at that time. My memories of the days and weeks leading up to this incident are very foggy. But I do know this. My dad was absolutely correct when he told me I was selfish. If I had been successful, my suicide would have destroyed too many lives of people who loved me.

I didn't have any clear answers, except that I didn't feel valued. I felt worthless and deeply flawed, like there was something wrong with me. These symptoms are quite a paradox because my daily actions did not show any depression. I was still into sports, dating girls, and even smiling. In fact, when I look back at old photos of myself at that age, it is impossible to see any depression at all.

There is something to learn from this both as a child and a parent. Those of us who suffer from depression are somehow able to navigate through our daily lives, expertly hiding our pain. Although my family was a close-knit one in that we did a lot of things together, one thing we did not do was openly discuss our feelings. I never remember my siblings and I sharing our feelings, especially those relating to our parents' arguments and our mom's excessive drinking.

This was part of our family dynamic, and I suspect that many other families lived in similar situations. My parents soon sent me to a counselor, but all that did was to reaffirm that something was wrong with me. Some readers may wonder, *"Why didn't you just tell someone?"* Are you kidding me? They obviously do not understand the overwhelming sense of guilt and shame that would manifest itself after an admission to others of wanting to end your life.

I have some more good news and bad news. The bad news is that I continued to suffer from depression for many years, (especially while attending college) and yet, I was somehow able to contain and manage it. The good news is that my life took an abrupt turn (age 40) after a weekend-long seminar called The Forum. It was at this workshop that I learned how to stop telling myself the same old story and that I could choose to create a new one.

This turned out to be a moment of epiphany for me. My pity party was now over. There were about 200 participants at this workshop, and all of us were there for different but similar reasons. One of the most eye-opening and life-changing suggestions we learned was the importance of making a choice. My not-so-complicated choice was, "Be sad…. or….be happy". Duh!

This choice, at that time, was so obvious. *Why didn't I know that?* The fact is that I didn't know that I had a choice. I felt 'stuck'. It was that simple. Part of my own personal growth was realizing that even if I had bad memories or thoughts occurring from time to time, I could still choose how long I wanted to hold on to them. After that seminar, my personal decision was to limit any negative thoughts or memories to five minutes (and then, four minutes, and so on).

After weeks of practice, I was able to leave the past in the past (where it belongs) and focus on having an unimaginable future for myself (which I did). I left this four-day conference proud of all of my accomplishments in life and I was ready for an exciting future. It is difficult to imagine and summarize all the things I would have missed by killing myself.

The rest of the stories in this book are just a few of those things that I would have never happened. But more importantly I would never have been a teacher. I would never have had that opportunity to change the lives of thousands of my students. Forty-seven years in the classroom gave me a lot of practice.

Taking my own life meant that I would never have met my wonderful friend and wife Vita and have enjoyed the unforgettable moments of raising our two incredible sons, Kevin and Chris.

I would never have created the many games and activities for the classroom which enriched the art of learning for my students. And then I also would not have had that chance to write my best-selling memoir, "One Student at a Time," and more recently my new memoir about my family and what it was like to grow up in the '50s and '60s.

I learned that dreams can and do come true. I still have plenty of dreams and it's these dreams that keep me going. For example, one day, I recall walking near a parked car on my way to play tennis, and it had a community college bumper sticker on its trunk. I immediately fantasized about teaching at that college. Guess what? Within one year, that daydream came true.

Here's another one. Many years later, my wife and I were driving around looking for a new home to live in. We visited a gated community and we both began to imagine what it would be like to live there. Sadly, it was way out of price range. Guess what? Within two years, we owned a home on their golf course. Don't ever stop dreaming.

Since my retirement from teaching (January 2015), I have been speaking to teachers around the country at educational conferences and colleges. And more recently, I have been invited to speak to school groups, including JHS, HS, and college. What is both therapeutic and rewarding is that my topic is usually "Making a Choice."

We Want Rand?

It's time to switch gears. I just remembered a funny story that happened in my junior year of HS. Our classmate and basketball teammate, Johnny Strand, shared the bench with Creighton and me. Johnny was awkward, lanky, and not a very good player. However, due to his awkwardness and great attitude, he became somewhat of a fan favorite and a folk legend to the rest of the school.

As usual, one night, my mom came to the game hoping I would finally get some playing time. By the time we reached the fourth quarter, our team was ahead by about 20 points creating hope that all of us on the bench would finally get into the game.

Suddenly, the standing room only crowd started chanting, "We want Strand…we want Strand." Our coach finally obliged, and Creighton, Johnny Strand, and I were sent into play. The crowd went crazy, especially when Johnny Strand made a basket.

After the game, I went to meet my mom. She looked at me with eyes that were bigger than her smile, and said, "Kenny, I am so proud of you". Confused, I said, "Why, Mom? I had only played one minute, and I didn't even score a point." Then my mother said, "Didn't you hear the entire school shouting for you to get into the game. We want Rand, we want Rand."

I think I laughed for the next 10 minutes, and I finally broke the news. "Mom, they were shouting, we want Strand, we want Strand. Not, we want Rand." Mom and I laughed and smiled all the way home.

• Mr. Shank

In our junior year, we had a new teacher in our school. **Mr. Shank** was our eleventh-grade English teacher and a recent graduate of Yale University and was probably one of the most brilliant teachers I ever had.

He was rather strange looking, in that he closely resembled the fictional literary character Ichabod Crane from the story of the

Headless Horseman in Washington Irving's book "The Legend of Sleepy Hollow." This is not a compliment.

Mr. Shank was more than just an English teacher. He made us 'think'. He was very critical of our errors, but he believed in second chances. I enjoyed Mr. Shank's teaching so much that I enrolled in his drama class during my senior year. A remember is first assignment to us, which was to write an essay titled, "My Place Under the Sun." And for the first time in my growing years, I was forced to think about my future. This was a difficult essay for me because I did not have a conscious clear path of what I wanted to do or who I wanted to be. After hours of struggling, I ended my essay by writing that as unsure and as unclear as my future goals were, I knew in my heart that I wanted to help people and make a difference in their lives.

As a side note, Mr. Shank was chosen by the students to be the chaperone for our senior trip to Washington, where he brought his wife along. It was shocking to see her beautiful movie star looks. My mind was constantly wondering how this unattractive man had managed to find such a lovely wife. I was too young and too shallow to understand that women were not just attracted to good looks. Not confident about my own appearance, I'm now thinking that I still have a chance with the opposite sex. More about that infamous senior trip later. My senior year is quickly approaching. I can't wait.

CHAPTER FIFTEEN

Senior Year 1962- 63

- **Elaine Grandolfi**

All throughout high school, I was a member of the Student Council. My dad told me, early in my high school career, that colleges are impressed by well-rounded students who have good grades, participate in activities, and are active in student government.

One of the members of the student council was a classmate named Elaine Grandolfi. Here is another one of my HS mysteries. Elaine hated me. No matter what suggestion I would make at a council meeting, she would vehemently disagree. I did my best to ignore her and remained polite to her, despite her apparent dislike for me.

At the beginning of our senior year, our class was going to have an election for 'Class President'. Elaine chose to run, and her opponent was another female student whose name I have since forgotten. Many of my closest friends disliked Elaine and encouraged me to run against her. They told me that the two girls would likely split the female vote and that I would probably win the male vote. Guess what? I won. It's no big deal, but it did look good on my college applications. Elaine never spoke to me again. Not even eye contact. Sore loser, huh?

• **Three of the Four Seasons**

Put on your seat belts. This is one of my all-time favorite stories. The year is 1962, and it is a week before Thanksgiving. I am only 16 years old and a senior at Ardsley High School. It's a typical Saturday night. I am with my friends Creighton and Mickey singing and harmonizing under a streetlamp directly in front of the old school, fantasizing about us being a famous singing group.

After we sang our favorite songs, we headed to the school dance party to grab some pizza and dance the night away. At about 10:30, an older friend, Stu Silverman, who had graduated a year earlier, came into the party and walked right up to the three of us.

Stu: "How you guys doin'?"
Me: "Great, what's up?"
Creighton: "Do you want to go jam somewhere?"

Stu was not a singer, but he did play the drums.

Stu: "You must have been reading my mind."
Mickey: "What do you mean?"
Stu: "Do you guys want to go to a nightclub tonight?"
Creighton, Mickey, and I: "Whaaaaat?"
Stu: I can get you into the 12:20 Club." The 12:20 Club was a night-
club on Central Avenue in White Plains, NY.
Me: "What are you talking about? We are all underage."
Stu: "There will be no problem getting you in. I know the owner."
Creighton: "Oh...Is this the place where the Billy Vera band plays?"
Mickey: "Holy shit. They are great. Billy Vera, the blue-eyed soul."
Stu: "So, what do you say? Let's do it."

On this cold November night, we hopped into Stu's car and drove to Central Ave. in White Plains, NY. We arrived about twenty minutes later.

Stu: "Guys, this is going to be great. Joe, the owner, is out in front, and I'll get you guys in." We all follow Stu to the front door. Meanwhile, we are trying to look older than we are, and then Stu shocks us when he says to the owner (now get ready for this. Are you sitting down?)

Stu: "Joe, I have a surprise for you. I want you to meet three of the Four Seasons."

The three of us are now thinking: *Holy _____. Did he really say that?*

Joe: "Wow...bring them in. I'll talk to Billy and get them on the stage.

Me: *Is this really happening?*

Frankie Valli and the Four Seasons were at that time probably the hottest singing group in the country and just had two #1 smash hits, "Sherry" and "Big Girls Don't Cry".

My head is spinning. Creighton, Mickey, and I are all looking at each other in disbelief. Fortunately, the Four Seasons had not made any personal TV appearances otherwise; we would not have been able to go through with this outlandish lie.

Billy Vera: "Ladies and gentlemen, we have a great surprise for you tonight. Are you ready to listen to the hottest signing group in America?" The crowd is going crazy. "Well, here they are, we are lucky to have three of the Four Seasons here with us tonight."

The packed nightclub of over 200 people went wild with excitement. Creighton, who has a great voice and can sing like a professional, is not shy about his talent and he turns to Billy Vera and asks him "Can you play 'In the Still of the Night?" Billy: "Are you kidding? That's one of my all-time favorites." Creighton turns around, winks at Mickey and me, and whispers, "Just try and sing backup for us just like you do on the street corner."

I must admit that Creighton and Billy were incredible. One song led to another, and then another, and in the next hour and a half, we sang almost every rock and roll hit ever made. It's now about 1:00 AM when Billy Vera came over to us and told us that they usually finished playing at this time, but the crowd was into the great music and singing. He said he wanted to continue playing and singing with us, but his band needed a short break.

During the break, people in the crowd came over and politely asked us for our autographs and they also kept asking us to sing the hit records of the Four Seasons. Although Creighton was a great singer, he did not possess the high falsetto voice of Frankie Valli, so we knew we would not be able to sing their songs as well as the original.

We made up a lie and told our excited and adoring fans that we were under license not to sing those songs without our lead singer. Creighton, Mickey, and I went outside during the break to get some fresh air, and Creighton quickly lit up a cigarette. A few minutes later, Stu came up to us with excited eyes.

Stu: "You're not going to believe this."
Me: "What?"
Creighton: "How did we do?"
Stu: "The owner loved it. He wants to invite all of you back next weekend (Thanksgiving weekend), and he is willing to pay each of you $1500 each per night."
Creighton: "$1500 WOW!" That was a lot of money at that time for two hours of singing."
Mickey (*with a smile from ear to ear*):" Holy _____ "
Stu: "What do you think?"
Creighton (also smiling from ear to ear): "Let's do it.
Me: "Wait, wait, wait. Are you kidding? Are you crazy? We can't do this. We are not part of the Four Seasons. We are impostors. No way."
Creighton: "They think we are. Ha"
Mickey: "I'm in."
Me: "We can't do this. This is out-and-out fraud. We'll get arrested."

Creighton: "Come on, Kenny. Don't we a wuss."
Me: "Well, you and Mickey can be two of the Four Seasons, but I'm out."

I wasn't even tempted to do this. During this outdoor discussion, we were all shivering because it was very cold outside. At this point, I didn't want to return to the nightclub. I was ready to leave and go home. Stu told us that he would tell the owner that we needed to check our calendar and that we would let him know as soon as possible.

While we were still outside, we could hear the crowd of admirers from the inside shouting; "We want more. We want more." So, by popular demand, the three of us then went back inside and continued singing with Billy Vera and his incredible band until about 2:00 AM. After we finished, we signed our phony autographs for some fans and laughed all the way home. After a few days of thought, my friends finally agreed that it would not be a good idea to perform there again. It was a good decision.

Just as a side note. Singer-songwriter Billy Vera had a very successful career, recording a No. 1 Billboard hit (1987) titled "At This Moment". He also wrote a No. 1 hit for Dolly Parton, and his band was featured in the Bruce Willis movie "Blind Date" and various TV shows. He also performed at the prestigious Apollo Theater and recently received a Hollywood Walk of Fame star.

He is, in my opinion, one of the most talented performers I have had the pleasure of seeing (and singing with, HA!). If that wasn't enough, he has also written a bestseller titled "From Harlem to Hollywood." And he's also a super nice guy. Below is a photo of Billy Vera, ("the Blue-Eyed Soul", and his band playing at the 12:20 club.

• **Nancy Brown**

I met Nancy Brown at a Dobbs Ferry High School sock-hop after one of their home basketball games. What's a 'sock-hop'? Keep reading you will soon understand Their school invited us the opposing team, to the dance, offering a truce to help ease our bitter rivalry. Nancy was one of the prettiest and most popular girls in Dobbs Ferry, and she instantly caught my eye.

I somehow found the courage to ask her to dance. Dancing was a comfortable and safe way for me to meet girls. I was too shy to approach a girl and start a conversation, so it was less of a risk for me to approach a girl and ask her, "Would you like to dance?" especially if they had already seen me dancing with someone else.

Of course, not all girls said, "yes". Ah, the pain of rejection. Nancy and I quickly hit it off, but not romantically. This was because she had an instant crush on my older brother, Binnie, who stole her and the show when he danced with her at this same sock-hop. I've always thought that Binnie was a better dancer than me, but my very partial HS friends disagreed.

Nancy and I remained friends throughout the next three years of high school. Her dating my brother was awkward, strange, and difficult for me because I had a huge crush on her. However, I remained loyal to my brother and to her.

Although she dated Binnie on and off for two years, Nancy and I would talk for hours each night, on our newly invented push-button phones. Finally, in my senior year, two years after Binnie graduated and stopped dating Nancy, I made my move. I learned from an earlier experience that one of the best ways to get a girl to notice me (romantically) was to leave her alone. Just ignore her. So, for one month, I stopped hanging out with her and I stopped speaking to her on the phone.

Having ignored her numerous phone calls, Nancy went out of her way to drive over to our home to talk to me. She was friends with our entire family, and my mom let her in. When Nancy saw me, she began to cry. She asked me, "What's wrong? Are you mad at me? What did I do?" I coldly said, "Nothing's wrong." She asked me if we could go for a ride, and I reluctantly said, "Yes."

During the car ride, she kept peppering me with questions about what was wrong. I finally told her that I was fed up with 'just' a friendship. She was shocked and said she didn't feel that we had a romantic connection. I got angry and asked her, "Am I ugly? Am I dumb? You love talking to me and dancing with me. Is that it?"

She looked confused and didn't know what to say. I angrily told her, "Take me home." She asked, "Are you willing to give up our friendship?" Once again, I said, "Just drive me home," which she reluctantly did. When I got home, I was hurt and angry and close to tears, but to my surprise, Nancy called me about an hour later. I tried to make a quick emotional recovery, and she unexpectedly asked me to come over to her house. I said, "What for?" and she said, "Just cover over; you won't be disappointed."

Well, I went over, and she was instantly all over me, kissing me, hugging me, and making out. After an eternity, she said, "You know what? You are a better kisser than your brother." We dated for the next two months, and then summer came, and I fell in love(?) with Ellen O'Brien. Teenagers can be very fickle. Curious as to how she is now doing, I have tried repeatedly to find her on social media, but no luck (yet).

• Are We Going to Die?

It is 1962, I am sadly not a serious student, and I know little, if anything, about history and current events. However, the rest of the people in the United States and I would soon get a reality check. In the middle of October, the American media was reporting extensive coverage that Russian missiles were photographed in Cuba, just 90 miles from the US.

I remember the newspaper photographs of the missiles, but my teenage eyes could not identify a missile from a fallen tree. Our entire country went on, what is now known as 'Red Alert'. On October 22nd, President Kennedy went on national TV and ordered a naval blockade around Cuban waters to prevent any more Soviet ships from bringing missiles carrying atomic bombs to Cuba.

For the first time in my life, the possibility of World War III became a frightening reality. I could not sleep that night knowing that Russian ships, loaded with missiles with nuclear war heads were heading toward Cuba and right toward the American blockade. The news coverage reported that the Russian vessels were set to intercept our blockade around 10:05 AM Eastern time the next morning.

At 9:45 AM, while sitting in my English class, the school sirens rang, indicating that the entire student body and teachers were to leave the classrooms and proceed to the hallways, bend down, and put our heads between our legs (and pray). I am sure that I was not the only person counting down the minutes and seconds, waiting and hoping.

At 10:06, the principal addressed the students over the loud-speakers and announced that the Russian ships had turned around. At which, the entire student body and teachers let out a loud roar of relief and approval. Everyone knew that if the Russians had been foolish enough to pass through the blockade, missiles from both countries would have been fired, and WWIII would have started (and ended humanity).

Even though the outcome was an instant relief, I had nightmares about WWIII for weeks, and in those dreams, I could see and hear the Russian missiles overhead. Us baby boomers are the first and only generation to have experienced an immediate fear that WWIII would begin the next day and be the end of civilization as we know it.

• The Man Who Saved the World

I am wondering how many of you have ever heard of Vasily Arkhipov? I am sure that most of you have not. During this missile crisis, he was the captain of a Russian nuclear submarine off the coast of Cuba. Not known to many, our ships off Cuba were dropping depth charges, hoping to destroy his submarine. His Russian commanders soon ordered him to launch missiles in retaliation.

Captain Arkhipow refused to do so and quickly moved his submarine away from Cuban waters. In 2002, Thomas S. Blanton, then director of the US National Security Archive, credited Arkhipov as "the man who saved the world". Scary huh?

• Me vs. Mr. Hester

It's my turn.

In 1962, I became a senior and tried out for the varsity basketball team, and of course, Mr. Hester, who had replaced Coach Jackman, was now the coach. You may remember that I made the team in my junior year. I was, of course, aware of the previous family incidents with Hester, but I had a great week of tryouts, playing better than most of my teammates.

When Hester posted the final list of players who made the team, I was shocked, angry, and frustrated to see that my name was not on the list. I'm not stupid. Our family's suspicion that he might have been antisemitic was becoming a reality. I was, however, able to get some revenge.

Towards the end of our senior school year, we had the annual senior/faculty basketball game. Mr. Hester, at 6'4", was the best of all the faculty players. We had about 25 senior players, and we decided to break up into five teams of five. Each of these teams would play for about six minutes, giving all of us a fair amount of time to play.

My four teammates and I all decided to wear Superman capes with a big letter "S" on our shirts.

We also formed a separate starting five (of which I was a part of) to play the first six minutes hoping to get us off to a good start. Guess who was guarding me. Mr. Hester, of course. My adrenaline instantly took over, and I was 'on fire'. During the game's first six minutes. I repeatedly made jump shots right over Hester, and when I wasn't scoring, I passed the ball and gave my teammates easy layups.

After those initial six minutes, we were winning 16 – 2. I scored eight points and had three assists. I was personally responsible for 14 of our 16 points. After graduating High School, I went on to play college freshman basketball, and I took both pride and revenge by sending him the newspaper articles, photographs, and box scores to Hester to show him that he was wrong.

• Mr. Braunhut

Much like the other teachers that I already acknowledged and admired, Mr. Braunhut, our senior year English teacher, had a flair for connecting with his students, except on this one unusual day, the Monday after our senior prom.

Let me set the stage for what was about to happen: Quite a few of us went to Jones Beach on Long Island, on Sunday, the day after the Saturday night prom. What this means is that on that Monday, we were mentally still at the beach. Almost everyone in the class was chatting about their fun experiences at the prom and at the beach, and the upcoming graduation.

We were so engrossed that we were inadvertently ignoring Mr. Braunhut as he entered the class. Out of the corner of my eye, I could see that he was getting somewhat annoyed at the constant talking. I noticed him as he was looking around the room with concern, and he finally said, "Ahem...Ahem," which everyone ignored.

He then went to the blackboard and wrote down a sentence. Again, no one paid attention, and again, he turned to the class, and said, this time a little louder, "Ahem...Ahem." Still no response. He then went to the blackboard on the side of the room near the front door and wrote the same sentence for the second time. And once again, there was no response.

I'm not sure why I was watching him so closely. Perhaps I was getting a kick out of him getting flustered and I could see that frustration increase as his face turned red with anger. After his failed attempts to get our attention, he went to the back of the room, where there was still another blackboard, and wrote the same sentence, now for the third time.

After this, he turned around and faced the class, saying quite loudly, "**Ahem...Ahem**." And still, no one noticed or paid attention (except for me). In anger, he then grabbed someone's textbooks from their desk in the back of the room and slammed them down onto the student›s desk.

The noise was so loud that we all stopped talking and stared at him in total silence. His face was a deep red and contorted with anger. He then shouted, "I am really angry at all of you. I wrote the same sentence, not once, not twice, but three times on the board, and not one of you looked and saw that I made a grammatical mistake each time.

Here it comes.

Upon which, I stood up and said, "Mr. Braunhut, I noticed, and I think you should keep writing it until you get it right". The entire class burst out laughing. He did not find this at all amusing, and he picked up a chair, threw it in my direction, and walked out of the room. WOW!!

The next day I saw him after class and apologized to him, and I was fortunate that he liked me and accepted my apology. I tried to explain to him that we were all hyped about the prom, the beach, and our pending graduation. He told me that he understood, but unfortunately, he was having a bad day, and instead of sharing our excitement, he was fixated on what he wanted to do that day.

I think you can tell from this story that I was somewhat of a class clown and found ways to inject humor into the learning process, which is something that I often tried to do when I became a teacher. Yes, I also had my own students who would try to be a class clown, but my personal experiences helped me find a way to go with the flow and not take it personally.

- **The Infamous Senior Trip to Washington, D.C.**

One of the highlights of senior year in high school was attending the prom. However, our school, Ardsley High School, had another highlight, which for those of us in the twelfth grade was a traditional senior trip to Washington, D.C.

This trip typically took place in early June, approximately one to two weeks before the graduation ceremony. The school promoted the trip as an 'educational' experience, but we seniors had another plan.

We left the high school on Thursday morning via two buses filled with approximately 80 students, two teachers, and two parent chaperones. When we arrived at our hotel in D.C., we all went to our pre-assigned rooms, with six students in each room.

After resting up, we had dinner and went on a late-night boat ride on the Potomac River. Our guide told us stories about George Washington's crossing of the Potomac during the Revolutionary War, and we silently listened, pretending to be interested, but we were very bored. We had dinner on the boat and were pleasantly surprised to find a band playing dance music.

To my delight, the night ended with a dance contest. We weren't the only school with students on this boat, and the dance floor was packed with about 50 couples, many of whom were from different parts of the country. I am pleased to say that my partner and I won first place. The first-place prize was five silver dollars each. Looking back, though it doesn't sound like much of a prize, it was pretty cool at that time, and there is something about 'winning' which is a prize in itself.

There is only so much sightseeing that hormonal teenagers can mentally and physically handle, so on the last night of the trip, two incidents became infamous. One was that my close friends and I decided to stay in our room (instead of going sightseeing), and they (not me) got drunk. I was not a drinker, but I stayed and took part in sharing stories.

Simultaneously, without our knowledge, about six of our female classmates decided to go skinny-dipping in the hotel pool. I should have gone swimming instead. The next morning, Mr. Shank, our chaperone, knocked on our hotel door, telling us it was time for breakfast. Later that day, he found a way to gather all of us together, and he verbally lashed out at us, especially the ladies who had gone skinny dipping.

He was upset that we had broken protocol and was concerned that we might have ruined this trip for future senior classes. When we returned home, the school administrators were informed about our misbehavior and announced to the school that all future senior trips would be canceled indefinitely. We were lucky that no one got suspended from school. For a very long time, we were the last senior class to go to Washington, D.C., or anywhere else.

• High School Graduation

I remember so little about graduation night that I almost left out this event from my book. No one farted and fell off their chairs and nothing special happened other than the emotional 'good-byes' and 'good luck' wishes. My mom had a party for me at our home with family, and all of my friends did the same. That's all folks. Of course, there is a sense of loss, and leaving memories behind, and there is also a sense of feeling lost. However, my close friends and I already had made plans for one last celebration.

• Boys' Night Out!

It is June 29th, 1963. Even though we had just graduated a few weeks prior and we had recently attended our prom and family graduation parties; my friends and I decided to have some closure to our high school days. In a few short months, Dave and Tommy would be off to Tufts University, I would be attending Fairleigh Dickinson University in New Jersey, Carl was going into the Army, and Creighton into the Navy. It made sense to all of us that one last boys' night out would be the best thing to do.

We all planned to meet at the outdoor pavilion near the McDowell Little League ballpark complex in Ardsley at 11:00 PM, bringing our own sleeping bags and liquor. I'm not sure what everyone did earlier on that Saturday evening, but Carl, Creighton, and I went bowling in White Plains, NY.

Around 10:30 PM, the three of us drove over to the park and walked a short distance to the pavilion. When we got there, we were a little surprised (maybe not) that Tommy, Dave, and another friend were already drinking heavily. There were over 12 full bottles of alcohol, including Scotch, Whiskey, gin, and vodka, as well as a case of beer and a substantial amount of wine. You name it, we had it.

Even with my disdain for alcohol, I decided to fit in. Peer pressure can be very persuasive. Within a short time, all six of us were plastered. This was the first time I ever drank alcohol, and for the first time in my life I got drunk. It is now about one AM in the morning, and the scent of alcohol could be smelled way beyond the pavilion. This is important because of what was going to happen next.

Suddenly, we saw some car lights heading towards the driveway leading to the park. Dave instantly shouts out, "Oh shit… that's my dad. He's looking for me. We can't let him find me here." We all started to scramble, and fortunately, we found, behind the pavilion, a wooded area with trees and shrubs. We looked at each other and knew what we had to do. We then buried Dave under some branches and leaves, and we did our best to hide him.

Thirty seconds later, Dave's dad walked up to the pavilion. "Where's Dave? Have you guys been drinking? Where's Dave? I know he's here." He then conducted a thorough search in and around the pavilion. While searching in the darkness behind the pavilion, he stepped right over Dave, who was buried under branches and leaves in the wooded area, and fortunately, Dave's dad didn't see him. Whew!

Dave's dad growled, left us, and drove home. My only thought was that I hoped his dad wouldn't beat him when he got home. We asked Dave, "What are you going to tell your dad?" He told us not to worry and that he would tell his dad he had slept over at his girl-friend's house. Good luck with that. The morning after, never mind, use your imagination.

The pavilion. (AKA our bar for the night).

- **More about Dave Reed (January 1964)**

As mentioned earlier, Creighton, Carl, Dave, Tommy, and I were all very close friends. It shouldn't be surprising that even a year after we graduated, all of us decided to spend New Year's Eve (1964) with each other. Some facts and memories are blurry, but we (including girls we knew) went to a party in Irvington, New York, which was only five miles north of Dobbs Ferry. Dave was there with his girl-friend Pam Patterson, and Creighton was with his girlfriend Carolyn Ramin. Carl. Tommy and I were there just to dance, drink, and have a good time.

Dave was unique. First of all, he was one of the brightest students in our class. And he was also very mischievous. Ardsley was a small town, and there were no safe secrets. At this New Year's Eve party, I decided to remain sober while all of my friends were getting drunk. I believe it was me who drove most of us home that night Except for Dave, who drove to the party in his sports car, a beautiful dark green MG. Most of us left the party around 1:00 AM.

The next morning, I was woken by a 6:00 AM phone call from one of the girls in our group, JoAnne Esposito.

JoAnne: "Kenny?"

When someone calls you at this early hour, it cannot be good news; however, I was not awake enough to totally comprehend what I was about to hear.

Me: "What's up? Why are you calling so early?"
JoAnne (crying): "Kenny...Dave is dead."

I went into immediate shock. I had been with him a few short hours earlier. While on the way home, he crashed his sports car MG into a tree in the town of Dobbs Ferry on Ashford Ave., just a mile from my home.

What a loss. So young, just 20 years old. Of course, there is a lot of mystery as to the cause of the crash, but those answers will not change anything. Our dear friend is gone. Someone brilliant once said, "As long as I am remembered, I will never die." Long live Dave Reed, you will always be remembered and loved. We are all unique in our own way, but he was truly "one of a kind".

• Drugs, Alcohol and Cigarettes

When I was in the 8th grade, most of my guy friends were smoking cigarettes almost every day. It's strange, but I do not remember any of our girlfriends being smokers. Peer pressure is indeed powerful, so I wanted to at least give it a try. So, for a very short time period, when I was with my friends, I would occasionally smoke while they were smoking.

One day, about two weeks after my first cigarette, a group of us were walking up Ashford Avenue on our way to play basketball at the old school. As I was walking and smoking, I began to realize how terrible the cigarette tasted. It was gross. I'm now thinking, *this is one of the stupidest things I have ever done.* I was receiving absolutely no pleasure from smoking this cigarette. I immediately took it out of my mouth, threw it on the pavement, and stepped on it to put it out.

One of my friends said, "Kenny, what are you doing? You are wasting a good cigarette"? I quickly told him, "There is nothing good about any cigarette". And that was it, my smoking days were over.

No one in our family, other than our mom, ever smoked. Mom was a heavy chain smoker; she would often go through three packs of cigarettes a day. The strange thing is that she never smoked an entire cigarette. Mom would smoke about half of it, put it in an ashtray, and then light up another one.?????

No one is our family ever took drugs, and I don't think anyone in our high school was taking drugs or smoking marijuana. If someone did, it was a well-kept secret.

Drinking was another story. My friends and I would frequent a bar in Dobbs Ferry. They would go there to have a beer (or two). I went there so I could be with my friends and have a great meatball sandwich served by the very cute Mary Ann, the owner's daughter. I really don't recall alcohol being at any of the house parties we went to. Our "Boys night out", was the first time I ever drank alcohol and the first and last time I ever got drunk.

CHAPTER SIXTEEN

Television, Movies, and Sports

Cultural Trivia

It's time to reflect on the really important things in life. Just kidding. Entertainment is a part of our great American culture. So, in keeping my promise to keep you up to date with our changing world, I hope you will find the following information to be both informative and nostalgic.

• **Television:**

We were living in a time when TV 'westerns' ruled the television airways. This included the hit shows such as *Gunsmoke, Wagon Train, The Rifleman, Have Gun – Will Travel, Bonanza*, and *Rawhide*. I'm not sure what spurred the rise of these 'cowboy westerns', but it was evident that the tastes of the American audience were changing. *Bonanza* was reportedly the highest-rated TV show in terms of viewership over a ten-year period.

The game show, "The Price is Right," first aired in 1959, hosted by Bob Parker, and remarkably is still on the air today, but is now hosted by comedian Drew Carey. TV game shows also became a cultural phenomenon.

In 1959, Congress held hearings regarding a major cheating scandal on two very popular TV quiz game shows. It appears that the producers of the shows, *The $64,000 Question* and *Twenty-One*, fed the answers to questions to the contestants to help increase interest in public viewing. This was a big deal in that both shows drew a large audience.

- **Late Night TV**

The late 1950s and early 1960s saw a dramatic rise in late-night television. These shows were pioneered by cigar-smoking comedian Ernie Kovacs (who is worthy of watching his crazy antics shown on YouTube). Kovac was soon followed by Steve Allen (1954-1957), then Jack Paar (1957–1962).

Steve Allen switched from ABC to NBC (1962-1964) and originated *The Tonight Show*. Johnny Carson took over for Steve Allen on ABC (1962) and, after a thirty-year career, passed the reins to Jay Leno.

All of the late-night shows were hosted by comedians and provided great entertainment. These talk shows were broadcast from Monday through Friday, after the late-night news (around 11:00 PM), when people were usually sleeping or engaging in intimate activities.

During this television time period, Johnny Carson frequently credited himself for the decrease in American births. Use your imagination. The quick witted and entertaining Carson loved to showcase other comedians such as Billy Crystal, Joan Rivers, and Buddy Hackett. If you haven't had a chance to see Billy Crystal's imitation of Muhammad Ali, it is worth the effort to go to YouTube and see a classic that should not be missed. An interesting fact is that all three of these comics had their roots in hotels in the Catskill Mountains in New York.

My personal favorite late-night host was Steve Allen. One reason is that he was very creative. Another reason was that he often had these weird guests, and a third reason was that he had these established routines that kept me laughing all night long. One of those routines was his parody of a TV news broadcaster. To begin this skit, he would take off his glasses, turn them upside down, and put them back on his face. I am laughing already. He would end his news parody with the nonsensical phrase "Smoock...Smoock," which became a daily mantra for me and my friends. Just a few months ago, I received an email from my best HS friend (Creighton) and he ended his email with, "Smoock, Smoock."

• **Movies**

The movie *Gigi* won the Academy Award for Best Picture. The remake of *A Night to Remember* was a hit movie, as was Alfred Hitchcock's *Vertigo,* starring Jimmy Stewart and actress Grace Kelly. The film *A Cat on a Hot Tin Roof,* starring Paul Newman, also helped launch the career of the beautiful and talented Elizabeth Taylor. A truly memorable movie was *Psycho,* starring the very convincing Anthony Perkins and actress Janet Leigh, directed by Alfred Hitchcock. No one who watched that movie will ever forget the brutal and frightening shower scene.

• **Newman and Redford**

The late 1950s and early 1960s witnessed the rise of several notable actors, with two of the best being Paul Newman and Robert Redford. Both were very handsome and talented. Newman and Redford were not only great actors, but also became Directors and Producers, winning numerous awards, including Oscars. And more importantly, they were philanthropists, donating millions of dollars to charity.

Paul Newman was in 52 movies as an actor. Two of my early favorites were *Somebody Upstairs Likes Me* (1956), in which he played middleweight contender Rocky Graziano, and the other, *Cool Hand Luke* (1967), in which there is a famous scene where he ate about 50 raw eggs. There is also a famous line from this movie when the prison warden tells him, after Newman repeatedly broke out of prison, "What we've got here is a failure to communicate." I'm laughing because I jokingly use that line numerous times in my own classes while teaching. Paul Newman passed away in 2008.

Paul Newman, for some people, may be best known for his salad dressing. What most people do not know is that he donated his entire profits from this venture to charity.

Robert Redford was about 10 years younger than Paul Newman, and he was in over 45 movies. There are too many great movies in which he starred and won awards for, but one of my early favorites was *Barefoot in the Park* (1967), in which he co-starred with actress Jane Fonda. I have seen this movie at least three times, and I still laugh at the same scenes even though I know what's coming.

Together, Newman and Redford starred in two of the most significant and iconic box office hits of all time. In 1969, they collaborated on *Butch Cassidy and the Sundance Kid,* and a few years later, they reunited for *"The Sting.*

Much like his friend Paul Newman, Redford was an activist and also donated heavily to charities. I was deeply saddened to learn that Robert Redford passed away yesterday. He was 89 years old.

Redford & Newman in the Sundance Kid.

• **Sports**

In 1960, heavyweight boxer Cassius Clay (Muhammad Ali) made his debut. His career got off to a slow start. The press nicknamed him the 'Louisville Lip" because he came across as extremely boastful and arrogant. The sporting media was not a big fan of Clay and often tried to discredit him. I recall reading articles that claimed he had a low IQ and was not fan friendly. But to me, he was a psychological genius.

Clay would often try to intimidate his opponents by having the audacity to predict the round in which he would knock them out. The big difference was that he was able to back up his words and fulfill his prophecies. At one press conference, he shouted out, "I am the greatest." This only added fuel to the flame about his arrogance, but guess what? He matched his words with his actions and was, in fact, the "Greatest of ALLLL Time."

CHAPTER SEVENTEEN

Music: Rock n' Roll 1958 – 1963

- **A Great List of Hit Songs**

Music, during the late 1950s and early 1960s, was a significant part of our teenage lives, and deserves its own chapter. Do you remember these great songs?

- "All I Have to Do is Dream" (Everly Bros)
- "Don't" (Elvis)
- "Tequila" (The Champs)
- "It's Only Make Believe" (Conway Twitty)
- "Get a Job (The Silhouettes)
- Just a Dream" (Jimmy Clanton)

And the list continues...

- "Sweet Little Sixteen" (Chuck Berry)
- "Book of Love" (The Monotones)
- "Short Shorts. Who wears short shorts?" The Royal Teens)
- "Great Balls of Fire" (Jerry Lee Lewis)
- "Donna", and "La Bamba," (Richie Valens)
- "Who's Sorry Now" (Connie Francis)

Who's sorry now?

Who's sorry now?
Whose heart is achin' for breakin' each vow?
Who's sad and blue? Who's cryin' too?

1958 was a particularly notable year for hit records. In this year. Elvis had three records in the top 50, and the Everly Brothers and Buddy Holly also had three top ten hits.

- **Ray Charles**

What an incredible iconic career. Mr. Ray Charles had over 80 (yes, 80) top ten Billboard hits from 1958 – 1990. His most famous songs are *Georgia on My Mind*, and *I Can't Stop Loving You*. The accolade of being a phenom or a genius is often overused, but Frank Sinatra has been quoted as saying that Ray Charles "is the only true genius in show business."

The talent of Ray Charles spanned numerous generations and genres, including Jazz, Country, Rock, and Blues. In 2004, actor Jamie Foxx starred in the biopic movie *Ray*, for which he won the Academy Award for Best Actor.

- **Alan Freed: Rock n Roll:**

From 1954 through 1959, disc jockey Alan Freed hosted over eighteen 'Rock 'n' roll' shows at the Paramount Theater in Brooklyn, NY. These shows were extremely popular among teenagers and drew huge crowds. (See photos below.) The one on the left is from one of the show's programs with a photo of Alan Freed.

I went to my first Rock 'n Roll show in 1958 with my brother Binnie. I remember being shocked that, despite leaving very early in the morning, a line of fans about six city blocks long had already formed with all of us hoping there would be enough tickets left to get in This was one of the many unforgettable experiences in my life.

This show featured the most popular singing stars in the world, such as Paul Anka, The Everly Brothers, The Platters, Frankie Lymon and the Teenagers, Chuck Berry, Bo Diddley, and many more. There was even a new Elvis Presley movie to watch. I clearly remember Mr. Freed announcing before the show began, "Please....no dancing in the aisles." That didn't work.

What I recently found to be very interesting is that in Freed's first show (Dec. 1954), Tony Bennett was the headline act. He was not a Rock 'n' Roll star, but he was the hottest singer at the time. In Freed's second show, the headline act was Count Basie, a noted jazz musician. His choice of headline acts for these shows changed abruptly after Elvis made seven appearances on the Ed Sullivan TV show. This illustrates how quickly the tastes of the American public can change.

- **Sock-Hops**

Immediately after our Friday night home basketball games, our school would sponsor a sock hop. This was a school dance tradition-ally held in the gymnasium, and because the school janitors did not want us to scruff up the floor with our shoes, we were asked to take off our shoes and dance in our socks.

During school dances in the late 50s and early 60s, it was very common for girls to sit or stand on one side of the gym, waiting to be asked to dance by a boy sitting on the other side. And it also wasn't unusual for my brother Binnie and me to be the first to ask a girl to dance. After about ten minutes of music with no one dancing, Binnie and I would catch each other's eye, and nod our heads, which signaled that it was time to get up and dance.

We would both then ask some girl to dance, and after entertaining our classmates for about five minutes, there would soon be over a hundred other students dancing. This happened almost every time there was a High School dance or Sock Hop.

- **Songs That Created New Dances**

Get ready for a cool trip down memory lane. Quite a few songs that we played at our HS sock-hops, dances, and home parties were songs that helped create a new style of dancing.

One of the first songs that I remember which created a new dance style was "The Stroll" (1958), sung by the Diamonds, who also had a massive hit with "Little Darlin". In dancing 'The Stroll', as often shown on the Dick Clark American Bandstand show, there were two lines of about 10-20 teenagers, with boys on one side and girls on the other side, standing about 8 feet apart. Then, you would take your partner on a dancing 'stroll' down the middle of the two lines, and another couple would follow shortly after. "The Stroll" had its own dance moves and style that we, as competitive and creative teenagers, would improvise to our own special moves and steps. I guess you can say that my generation invented the first 'line dance'.

Teenagers dancing 'the stroll' as seen On American Bandstand.

Now here is a song that created one of the biggest dance crazes of all time.

Come on, baby
Let's do the twist
Come on, baby
Let's do the twist
Take me by my little hand
And go like this

That's right, "The Twist." Initially recorded by Hank Ballard and the Midnighters (I did not know that), was later covered in 1960 by Ernest Evans (aka; Chubby Checker), and it remains popular today. I danced to the 'Twist' so many times in my life that my side still hurts.

Chubby Checker does not appear to look so chubby.

Other songs that created new dance styles were "Mashed Potato Time" (1962), and there was also "Do the Locomotion" (also 1962), sung by Little Eva.

- **Do you want to 'Shout'?**

Get ready for another cultural phenomenon. It was in July of 1959 when the Isley Brothers recorded the song "Shout. I clearly recall being at a school sock hop after a home basketball game. There were about 200 of us from different grades waiting for the music to start. When this song came on, we would quickly and almost uncontrollably become dancing zombies. It was seven minutes (if they played both sides) of mayhem, and even the shy students danced. It's somewhat reminiscent of the famous scene in the movie Footloose but to me, our dance looked more like a Southern church revival.

What is remarkable is that, over 50 years later, the song "Shout" remains one of the most popular songs at wedding celebrations. Come on, get up and get ready to dance.

Well...Now waaaitttt a minute
You know you make me wanna (shout)
Kick my heels up and (shout)

Throw my hands up and (shout)
Throw my head back and (shout)
Come on now (shout)
Don't forget to say you will
Don't forget to say yeah, yeah, yeah, yeah, yeah

Can you imagine what it was like to hear and watch over 200 obsessed teenagers singing and 'shouting' these lyrics as loud as they can and zombie dancing at the same time? One year later, the Isley Brothers released another hit record, "Twist and Shout," which became a mega hit when the Beatles covered it in 1963.

• **American Bandstand:**

I would be remiss if I didn't share with you the cultural experience that helped define the '50s and '60s. In 1956, *Bandstand* was a tri-state TV dance show, broadcast in New York, New Jersey, and Pennsylvania. In 1957, radio disc jockey Dick Clark took over the show, which then became a national TV show in August of that year.

Dick Clark, whose love for teenagers, along with his warm and inviting personality, became a national icon. He played the latest hit records, but he was also known for introducing new songs and new artists on his show. The show originally aired on Saturday nights, but soon became a daily afternoon show at 3:00 PM. Brilliantly aired at an hour when most teenagers were coming home from school.

One of the staples of his show was when he would get three teenagers to rate a new record. Their rating became a benchmark for the recording's success (or failure). It struck me, and the rest of the national audience, as a humorous moment when his conversations often went like this.

Dick Clark: "So, young man, how would you rate this song?"
Teenager: "I'd give it a 98%"
Dick Clark: "Oh...so you liked it. What did you like about it?"
Teenager: "It had a great beat, was easy to dance to, and the story behind the song was meaningful to me."

Dick Clark: "So tell me, would you buy it?"
Teenager: "No."

Dick Clark (and the entire national viewing audience), would laugh, at this all-too-common nonsensical answer.

American Bandstand went off the air in 2002 after breaking the record for the longest-running national TV show with over 3000 episodes. Soon after, Dick Clark became the host for the annual live New Year's party held in Times Square, in New York City.

I really miss watching Dick Clarkl's
American Bandstand

- **Singing Groups**

There were quite a few singing groups that were very popular in the late 50s and early 60s, and there were a few groups in particular that monopolized the radio stations. Let's see how good your memory is.

The Four Tops

This group had numerous hits for Motown Records, including, "Baby, I Need Your Loving", "I Can't Help Myself", "It's The Same Old Song", "Sugar Pie Honeybunch", "Reach Out I'll Be There", and so many more The Four Tops were known for their stylish moves and songs that were great to dance to. I can hear those rhythmic piano notes now:

Ohh...Sugar pie, honey bunch
You know that I love you
I can't help myself
I love you and nobody else

The Temptations

Led by lead singer David Ruffin, The Temptations also had a string of major hits including," Papa Was A Rolling Stone"," Just My Imagination", "Ball of Confusion", "Ain't Too Proud to Beg", "*My Girl*", and many more. Like their friendly rivals, the Four Tops, they were also known for their stylish dance moves and exciting performances.

The Coasters

Their hits included "Yakety Yak", "Charlie Brown", and "Young Blood". Most of their hits had what I call 'fun' lyrics that would bring a smile to your face as you sang along with your friends while listening to them on the car radio.

The Drifters

Their lead singer was Clyde McPhatter, and their hits include "There Goes My Baby", This Magic Moment", "Under the Boardwalk", and "Stand by Me." This last song became even more popular when it was featured in the movie by the same name.

Dion and the Belmonts

Their hit records include "Ruby Baby", "Where or When", Lonely Teenager", "The Wanderer", and "I Wonder Why", and "A Teenager in Love."

Each time we have a quarrel
It almost breaks my heart
'Cause I'm so afraid
That we will have to part...

• **Some Tragic News:**

On February 3, of 1959, a tragic a plane crash in Iowa killed rock 'n' roll pioneers Buddy Holly, Ritchie Valens, and J. P. "The Big Bopper" Richardson. I remember riding in my friend's car, listening to the radio when they announced the accident. First there was shock and soon the tears started to flow.

This horrible event is known as "The Day the Music Died" and was immortalized in Don McLean's 1972 hit song "American Pie". The world of music, especially for us young teenagers, went into instant mourning with a deep sense of loss for what we experienced and what could have been.

Left to right: Big Booper, Richie Valens, and Buddy Holly.

I don't know about you, but after listing these great singing groups and their hits, I can't help but feel nostalgic. I can clearly remember specific times and places when I first listened and danced to all of them. There is something special about music, (any kind of music), that allows us to do this. Not only are our memories individual, but they also have a sense of connecting us to our past experiences at a specific time in our lives. I am not assuming that all of us feel this way but there is something about our collective high school experiences that for every generation makes us feel that these were the best days of our lives.

I don't think we had the ability to realize this when we were there, but it is difficult to see and feel what it is like while being in the fishbowl. It is only when we are outside looking in when we are able to process and appreciate how great they were.

- **What's Next?**

College is soon approaching, but for me, it will have its own set of challenges. Before I share some of my amazing stories, I have some great tales of the summers at Brown's Hotel that took place during my teenage years. I don't know about you, but even with so much going on in high school it seemed that I was just passing time waiting for our summers to come.

My HS yearbook photo.

What happened to my curls? And my ears are not sticking out. Watch out Hollywood, here I come. By the way, I now have the nickname of "Hollywood". Long Story.

CHAPTER EIGHTEEN

My High School Summers at Brown's Hotel

Once again, my summers were a great opportunity to spend more time with my family, especially dad. But it was also a time of growing independence, and I soon began to have my own friends and adventures. These particular summers (1958 to 1963) turned out to be very special as you will read in some of my 'hard to believe' stories.

My dad, due to his excellent reputation, had a lot of leverage with the hotel owners, Charles and Lillian Brown. This leverage entitled our entire family (and we had a big family), to eat in the staff dining room. Eating daily at the staff dining room saved dad at least $200 a week.

The main dining room was massive and could seat and feed 1200 guests. It took a lot of food to feed 1200 people, and one of the weekly comics performing at the hotel had a standard joke about the guests and their dining room eating habits.

Comedian: "Mrs. Brown, is the hotel full?"

Mrs. Brown: "Oh yes, it is, we have 1200 people."

Comedian: "Oh, is that true? Your husband, Mr. Brown, told me that according to the dinner orders, you have over 5,000 people staying here.

Let's just say that the food was really good. Some years later, my dad was again able to negotiate with the Browns and finally obtained a guest room for himself and my mom, as well as a second room for any family member who decided to visit for the weekend. And dad's growing status led to both him and mom enjoying meals as guests in the main dining room.

- **Mr. "T"**

When I reminisce about Brown's Hotel, I have very fond memories of the hotel's flamboyant athletic director, Sam Tolkoff (aka Mr. T). Sam's full-time yearly job, outside of the summer, was as a teacher and coach of many sports, primarily basketball, at James Monroe HS in the Bronx, New York.

It wasn't unusual for New York City teachers to work in the Catskills each summer to earn extra money. It was obvious to those who knew him that Sam did not work at Brown's for the money. Sam was a busy man who also worked the winter holidays at the Miami Beach Doral Country Club where he befriended the great tennis player Arthur Ashe, and Hall of Fame baseball player, my sports hero, Willie Mays.

Sam's persona made him larger than life. He loved people and was great at his job. He did his best to plan day-long activities for the 1200 guests, and he was loved by all who knew him. Each day at the hotel, Sam posted a list of hourly activities that catered to all ages. These included horseback riding, basketball, volleyball, and softball games. Then there was his daily and entertaining calisthenics at the pool, where people of all ages exercised to his rhythmic army verses of "Go to your left, your right, your left…" And he often used music to make exercising routines more enjoyable and engaging.

To me, he was a friend and a mentor who helped improve my basketball skills and taught me essential life lessons. He advised me to never let anyone intimidate me and to have confidence, even if I needed to fake it. And I am pretty sure that he had this effect on almost everyone he met. It was due to his instruction and advice that I was able to have the skills and confidence to make the college basketball team.

Among the daily activities at the hotel was a staff - vs.- guests' basketball game. He never played in the hotel basketball game, but he put on a show during halftime by sitting in a beach chair and making a 40-foot half-court shot (every day) while still sitting in the chair on the side of the court. I never saw him miss a shot.

Sam wasn't your ordinary human being. He was special. Sam dedicated his entire life to improving his students' future and ensuring that the summer hotel guests had a memorable experience.

Mr. 'T' doing what he does best. Entertaining the quests by the pool.

Over the years, Mr. T. formed a bond with the entertainer Jerry Lewis. It should be no surprise that these two larger-than-life personalities hit it off and became friends. This led to Mr. T. hiring Jerry Lewis's son, Ronnie Lewis, to work on the hotel's athletic staff. I am told that Jerry Lewis even invited Mr. T. to fly with him on his private jet. Thank you for everything, Sam.

• Country

One summer, Sam invited one of his students (who's nickname was 'Country'), to work for him at the hotel. Sam would often fill his staff at the hotel with current and former students. He did this because he wanted to show them that there was a better life than the one, they were living in in the South Bronx. Due to Sam's efforts and connections, at least 50 of his students were able to obtain college scholarships.

Country's birth name was unknown to me at that time, but I later found out that his real name was Walter Bridges. Country originally lived in North Carolina, and he carried his southern accent with him when he moved to the Bronx. It wasn't long before, because of his heavy accent, that he inherited the nickname of 'Country'.

Country and I were about the same age, and we hit it off and became buddies. We did everything together—basketball, softball, dancing with the ladies, and hanging out. I felt like he was my brother, even though he was as black as night. Here is an interesting side story involving racism against my friend Country.

One day, we went on a short trip, about six miles away, to Liberty, New York. While we were there, we went to a luncheonette to order an Egg cream soda. So…what is an Egg cream, you ask? An Egg cream is a soda that is a specialty drink of New York, consisting of chocolate (or vanilla) syrup, a small amount of milk, and seltzer water (and no egg).

Anyway, when Country and I ordered our Egg creams, the middle aged and bald server behind the counter said, "Sorry, but we don't serve any n…….s in our store." Remember, this is upstate New York, not Mississippi. This was my first experience of blatant racism in New York, and I was shocked. I could sense that Country's entire body went into 'fight' mode, and I whispered to him, "Let me handle this.". I could see every muscle in Country's face and arms tighten up, and I told him. "Trust me, I got it."

I told the server, "Well, can I still get my chocolate Egg cream?" Country looked at me as if I were crazy. The server nodded yes and walked away. Country again looked at me and said, "What the "f "are you doing?" I looked back at him and just smiled, and again said, "trust me". Instantly, Country knew I had a plan.

The server soon came back and gave me my Egg cream. I began to drink it and said, "Wow, this is probably the best Egg cream I've ever had." The server smiled, and then I turned to Country and asked him if he wanted a sip of my drink. The server's face turned bright red with rage. Before Country took a sip, I turned back to the server, and as I did so, I 'accidentally' spilled the rest of my drink all over the server. I quickly and facetiously said, "I'm so sorry. That's a shame." And Country and I immediately walked out of the store.

Country looked at me and said, "You're my man." And we both laughed. We didn't fear retribution from the server because I believe that people like him were cowards. Also, both Country and I were significantly bigger than he was.

• Jerry Lewis

Here is a Jerry Lewis story that I hope you enjoy. I was about 15 years old and working (illegally) as a busboy in the coffee shop which was near the show theater. Usually, after the show, which ended around 11:00 PM, hotel guests would take the short 50-foot walk and pile into the nearby theater coffee shop for a late-night snack. The coffee shop was average size and held about 100 people. On this evening, however, because Jerry Lewis had just performed for two hours, there were over 200 guests in the coffee shop.

This summer, my job was to work in the coffee shop kitchen as a busboy, retrieving clean plates from the kitchen area to bring them out to the waiters and waitresses. It was a very busy night, and I was in a hurry to bring out the cups and saucers and didn't notice that the person who washed the dishes did not distribute the weight of the dishes evenly. As I walked from the kitchen door into the coffee shop, I could feel the plates begin to slide.

Guess who walked into the jam-packed coffee shop the second I entered from the kitchen doors. Yes. Jerry Lewis was walking down the four steps leading into the coffee shop to sit and relax and have some coffee and cake with Mr. & Mrs. Brown.

The applause and reception he received while walking down the steps was overwhelming. At that very moment, as I was walking from the kitchen into the coffee shop, I dropped the slippery bus tray of dishes that I was carrying on my shoulder. All of the dishes fell onto the floor and broke into a little pieces. The noise of the dishes breaking sounded louder than anything I wanted to hear. It was so loud that everyone stopped gawking at Jerry Lewis, and all eyes went to the source of the noise (me).

I quickly ducked down (hoping to disappear) and I began to pick up the pieces of the broken plates (I was too embarrassed to show my face). Jerry Lewis, being the comic genius he was, took advantage of this opportunity and shouted out, "Don't worry, kid… that's how I got my start," and everyone laughed (except me)—end of the story. Thanks to Jerry Lewis, I was not fired. I have one more Jerry Lewis story, and it is Part V of this book.

- **My Four Other Summer Jobs**

Job #1:

After that embarrassing incident in the coffee shop with the broken dishes, I was promoted to being a soda jerk. Now that I think about it, the word jerk is probably an appropriate word, and I don't think this job was a promotion. They probably just wanted to get me out of the kitchen.

It was early in the afternoon on a beautiful summer day, and the shop was busy and crowded, with orders for food and sodas coming in quickly from the guests. It is somewhat strange that the guests in the coffee shop had recently finished lunch in the dining room about an hour ago. *How could they still be hungry?*

My job was to serve people that were sitting at the counter who didn't want to wait to sit at a table. *I heard someone ask for help and went to find out what he wanted.* A chunky middle-aged man with wavy gray air was sitting down and he asked me for a chocolate milkshake, which I made for him in record speed.

After one sip of the milkshake, the customer voraciously spat out the contents from his mouth and said, "This is the worst-tasting thing I have ever had in my life." He looked straight at me and repeatedly said, "Drink it.... Drink it," as if he wanted some confirmation of how bad it was. Either that or he wanted to punish me. Well... I took a sip, and he was right. It was absolutely terrible.

I couldn't imagine what I had done wrong until I looked under the counter where I had got the milk and embarrassingly noticed it was not regular milk but non-pasteurized milk. If you have never had non-pasteurized milk, save yourself some agony and don't even try it. It tastes like vomit. YUK. All I could do was apologize and give him another milkshake (for free). I think I held that job for only three weeks.

Job #2

My brother Frankie owned a boat that he docked at the Lake in the small town of Loch Sheldrake which was only about five miles from the hotel. Frankie was hired at the lake to help rent motorboats and water skis and maintain the other boats.

Our family spent a lot of time there and Frankie taught me how to waterski and soon hired me to help him with customers. One day, Frankie had an errand to do and he left me in charge. Big mistake. As bad luck would have it, a family who rented a boat got stuck out on the lake when their engine died. I was the only one there who could help, so I took out an unused motorboat to go and rescue them. Not being an expert boat captain, I ran my boat into theirs, damaging both boats and their engines. Time to find a new job.

Job #3

The nearby small town of Loch Sheldrake also had a movie theater. One day, soon after the boat incident, I happened to walk by the theater and saw a "Help Wanted" sign. I asked the person at the ticket counter about it, and I was quickly hired as an usher. There was one major problem. The manager was about 90% deaf, which made communicating with her a daily challenge.

About a week later, the theater showed the popular war movie "The Longest Day." Not only was it the longest day, but it was also the longest movie, clocking in at over three hours. About halfway through the first showing of the movie, the sound went off. I waited with the customers for about 15 minutes, hoping the sound would go back on, but no such luck.

The customers started to leave, so I asked them to wait a few minutes to give me time to ask the manager to correct the problem. I immediately went upstairs and informed the manager, who was running the film room, that the sound had gone off. Evidently, she did not hear me, because the sound never returned, and the entire audience soon left the theater.

About thirty minutes later, the deaf manager came down from the film booth and saw the empty theater. She started yelling and screaming at me. I again tried to tell her about the sound not working, but to no avail. Still angry, she said, "You're fired".

Time to find another job. Which I unexpectedly did. My brother Binnie and I were soon hired as professional dancers.

• **Job #4**

Every summer on Wednesday nights at the nearby Kutcher's Country Club (Hotel) in the Catskills, was Mambo Night. All the best dancers and dance teams in the Catskill resorts would put on a two-hour show, displaying their dancing talents. The focus was not just on dancing the Mambo, but they would perform all of the Latin dances, including American freestyle.

Late in the summer of 1961, Linda Renee from the Brown's Hotel dance team approached my brother Binnie and me and invited us to show our talents on Mambo Night. And she also said we would get paid. I guess that now made us professional dancers.

Binnie and I had practiced together as a team (for years), and we already had some great dance routines. The competition was held in a small nightclub that had good sized stage and there were about 250 people in the audience.

All of the dancers were given about fifteen minutes to go on stage and do their thing. When Binnie and I danced our well rehearsed routines, we were quickly embraced by the audience and probably had more fun than they did. Our routines were a display dancing side by side showing our synchronicity and individual styles.

The best part was not the small amount of money. The best part was learning new moves and techniques from some very talented dancers. The entire evening was a friendly competition, culminating in a Mambo dance where every dancer and team took the stage simultaneously for a 'dance off ', with a grand prize of $500.

Binnie and I were shocked when we won the last dance competition, and we were asked to come back every Wednesday night for the rest of the summer.

This evening was spectacular in that it showed a diverse range of talent and dance styles. Our success on those nights helped to build our confidence to a point where we were ready to try our moves at the Big Apple (New York City) dance clubs. Stories for another time (and another memoir?).

Iris Teitzman

It is the summer of 1962. Most of the new hotel guests arrived on Sunday. There were many Sundays when I often sat on a comfortable chair on the hotel porch, watching the long line of cars dropping off families eager to begin their one-week vacation.

Every week, young and attractive girls would arrive with their families, making my summers a lot of fun, but none of them could compare to Iris Teitzman. My heart stopped on this one Sunday when I saw her get out of her family's car. There was, however, a significant problem. I wasn't the only one 'searching.' Within seconds, the entire valet staff and lunch staff were there to greet her. It was as if she were a famous movie star, and she quickly developed a huge entourage.

Iris was 16 years old (my age), and she had beautiful long blonde wavy hair and bright blue eyes. She was about 5'5" and had a beautiful shape. And she was wearing short shorts to emphasize it. If I had to compare her, I would say that she was a prettier, sexier, and younger version of Jennifer Aniston.

There was one major obstacle for me. How would an awkward 16-year-old teenager like me, who lacked confidence, compete with this entourage of good-looking 18 -to 21-year-old guys constantly surrounding her? This group of young men grew even more prominent when she went to the pool for the first time.

I was heartbroken, and I didn't even know her. What to do? What to do. Everywhere she went, whether in the hotel lobby, the pool, or the nightclub theater, Iris had this group of 10 – 20 young men constantly surrounding her.

The next day, my dad noticed that I had a sad look on my face. He asked me what was wrong, and I told him about Iris. I asked him what I could possibly do to get her attention. His response surprised me. He told me to ignore her. He went on to say that if she walked by me, I should look away and walk in a different direction, never making eye contact with her.

My mind was puzzled. How was this going to help? He told me that beautiful women hate to be ignored. He also told me, "Try to make it a point to talk to other girls when she is nearby. What do you have to lose?"

For the next few days, I did exactly what my dad told me to do. However, it didn't seem to be working. I was getting increasingly frustrated and heartbroken. The weekend was soon approaching, and there were only three days left before her weeklong stay was over.

On Friday night, feeling sad and confused, I went to the evening theater show and sat down at a table all by myself. While sitting there with my head in the clouds, I suddenly felt a tap on my shoulder. I looked up, and there she was. My heart almost flew out of my chest.

I somehow mustered the courage to say "Hi," and her first words out of her mouth, to my total astonishment, were, "Why don't you like me?" *(My dad was right)*. I told her that I didn't know her not to like her. She then asked me if it would be okay for her to sit down next to me, and of course, I couldn't refuse (my heart was pounding so loudly). Even though I already knew her name, I said, "I'm Ken;

what's your name?" She said, "I already know your name. My name is Iris. You're the band leader's son, right?" She then told me she had a crush on me for the entire week (BaBoom.... BaBoom), can you hear my heart beating?)

She was confused about why I never talked to her. I told her that I also had a crush on her, but that getting through the entourage surrounding her would have been like breaking into a guarded bank. She laughed and then asked me to dance (YES!!). Here was my chance to show my skills. It so happened that we danced a few feet away from my dad while he was playing the piano. I looked at dad with a big smile. Dad returns the smile with some raised eyebrows Which meant, "Way to go Kenny".

Iris became my girlfriend (for the next two days). After the weekend, she went home, and my heart was in teenage heaven, but you can imagine that I was also sad that she was leaving and that I would not see her for the rest of the summer (three more weeks). We kept in touch over the next few weeks, and when the summer ended, I asked her if I could come down to Brooklyn to see her. She told me that she now had a new boyfriend. Heartbreak. OUCH!

But I did learn something that summer. One thing was that I had a newfound confidence in myself. This charismatic and beautiful young lady chose me among all the young men at the hotel. And I also learned that my dad was a very smart man. You would think that this newfound confidence would help, but sadly, I just had too much baggage for it to make a change in my self-image.

• "SLEEP"

This is one of my favorite stories, and it is about a unique experience I had when I was the entertainer at a hotel show. So, did I get your attention?

It was a Thursday evening, and the theater club would not be having its normal show with the usual three acts: a dance team, a singer, and a comedian. On this evening, there was only one entertainer, and he was a hypnotist/comedian.

After introducing himself to the audience, he offered a disclaimer: "Under no circumstances will anyone who volunteers to come up on the stage do anything to hurt anyone or themselves. We are here to have some fun, so now, are there any volunteers?"

Slowly but surely, hotel guests, from the audience of about 800 people, began to volunteer and were asked to come on the stage. After about 15 of them were on the stage, the hypnotist announced he would like to have just one more volunteer. I was sitting with my friends, who kept egging me on. However, I thought that at 16, I was probably too young to be in the show. Suddenly, one of my friends grabbed my arm and raised it up as if I were volunteering. The hypnotist said, "Great, it looks like we have one more. Let's give him a round of applause."

I reluctantly made my way to the stage being somewhat hesitant to be on a stage full of adults, but I decided to just go with the flow. The hypnotist began his standard routine of trying to hypnotize us, which goes something like this:

"Look at my moving watch. You will soon become very tired. Keep looking. You are now falling asleep. Don't fight it. "(I'd better stop before I put my readers to sleep).

Surprisingly, I was quickly hypnotized, but strangely, I could hear every word the hypnotist said even though I was 'out.' He then said, "You will wake up when I count to three. One, two, three." I quickly woke up along with the other participants. The hypnotist was able to hypnotize about half of us, and those who weren't under his spell were asked to leave the stage.

He then gave those of us who were still on the stage a small index card and instructed us not to turn it over until he gave us the command to do so. "When I count to three, you will all turn over the cards and read the command. "One... two...three." I turned over the card, and all it said in large bold capital letters was 'SLEEP. I instantly went back into my hypnotic sleep.

He turned to the audience and said, "do you want to have some fun?" Of course, the audience enthusiastically responded "YEAH". He then gave us what is called a post-hypnotic suggestion. "When I count to three, you will all become a washing machine. "One...

two…three." And then, my entire body, arms, legs, chest, and head, were uncontrollably shaking. I could hear the audience laughing in unison.

Then the hypnotist spoke, "When I say "Off " you will all immediately wake up. He paused and said, "OFF," and I woke up. Apparently, four of the remaining eight participants were embarrassed and asked the hypnotist to leave the stage.

Now, I am one of the four volunteers still on stage. This next part is "R- rated." The hypnotist put us under his spell again, and a minute later, I heard him speaking to one of the male volunteers, "Who is your favorite actress?" The hotel guest answered quickly, "Bridgitte Bardot." I was not a 'visual' witness to what happened next and can only tell you what I heard and was told.

By the way, Brigitte Bardot was a very popular and sexy movie actress at that time. The hypnotist said, "Good choice. It just so happens that Brigitte Bardot is here tonight." He then asked his assistant to bring her out. What she brought out was a full-size plastic female blow-up doll. "Tonight is your lucky night. Miss Bardot wants you to make passionate love to her."

And with that, the hypnotist put the plastic doll on the man's lap, and the man started to kiss and touch (her) it all over her plastic body. The audience erupted with hysterical laughter. Through the laughter, I could hear a female voice shouting, "STOP…STOP." I was told after the show that his wife ran up to the stage, grabbed her husband, and led him out of the theater. I could hear the audience loudly laughing.

I soon became the focus of the hypnotist's act and was now the only one left on the stage. While still under his spell, he told me that the show was now over, and when he woke me up, I would not be able to leave the stage because I would be frozen to the floor. "One… two…. three… wake up." I was now wide awake, and he said to me, "Thank you so much for volunteering; you may now leave." He came over to me, stood about three feet away, and held out my coat jacket for me to take. I tried to reach for my coat, but my feet were frozen to the floor. The audience, of course, laughed at my struggle. He finally handed me my jacket and said again, "You can now leave; the show is over. He turned to the audience and said, "Let's have a round of applause for this young man." He turned to me and said, "Go ahead, you can leave," and again, I could not move my legs. More laughter.

He soon looked at me and said the magic word, "SLEEP." What happened next is somewhat unbelievable, but it is all true (and it is not R-rated). While I was under his spell, he said, "I am going to ask you to follow some commands, and I need you to trust me that you will not be hurt. Do you trust me?" I replied, "Yes." "When I count to three, your entire body will become as stiff as a board. One... two...three." And, of course, my entire body became stiff.

"Now, I want you to fall backward. I will catch you. FALL." I fell backward, and he caught me in his arms. I then heard a chair sliding near me, and he took my upper body (shoulder and head) and placed them on the chair. He asked the assistant for another chair, and she placed my feet, from the ankles down, on it. Hopefully, you can envision that there was nothing but empty space under the rest of my body.

He then turned to the audience. "I need everyone to be absolutely silent, and do not worry; he will not be hurt." I could hear another chair slide near me, and the hypnotist took off his shoes and stood up on the chair. He then took out a handkerchief and put it on my shirt.

Get ready for this. He then stepped on my chest and faced the audience. Again, there was nothing under me for support. I did not feel a thing. I was like a wooden board. I could hear the audience quietly respond in awe at what he did. He then made some jokes while he was standing on top of me.

A few minutes later, he and his assistant helped me become vertical again, woke me up, and he asked how I felt. I said, "Fine." The audience was utterly amazed by what they witnessed. Though I was quite aware of what happened, I did not feel any pain or soreness from the weight of this rather large man—a truly amazing experience. This was not some magical trick or illusion, it happened exactly as described So...my friends, hypnosis is real. Very real.

The summer of 1963 is over, and it was a fantastic summer. The question now is, how will this somewhat shy, insecure, and immature 17-year-old adapt and be ready for college? I am very apprehensive.

BREAKING NEWS 1959 - 1963!

Did you know that in 1959

- The population of the U.S. is now 178 million people.
- Fidel Castro's revolutionary army defeats Batista's government and takes control over Cuba.
- Alaska and Hawaii have become states.
- The invention of the microchip is the beginning of a technological change in the way we live.
- The first American soldiers are killed in the Vietnam War.

1960

- The first live TV presidential debate has a strong impact on the election between Richard Nixon and John Kennedy.
- Pilot Francis Gary Powers is captured by Russians after his U-2 spy plane is shot down.

1961

- The U.S. attempt to overthrow Fidel Caston in the Bay of Pigs (Cuba) fails.
- The Berlin Wall is built separating the city into two parts, stopping the flow of refugees fleeing communist East Berlin to democratic West Berlin.
- Russian cosmonaut Yuri Gagarin becomes the first human to orbit the earth.
- John F. Kennedy is now the President of the U.S.

1962

- Marilyn Monroe, mysteriously, dies at the age of 36
- John Glenn becomes the first American to orbit the earth.
- Beatlemania runs wild in Great Britain
- Valentina Tereshkova becomes the first woman in space.

Famous People Born:

- 1959: Simon Cowell, Hugh Laurie, Brian Adams, Magic Johnson
- 1960: Sean Penn, Cal Ripken Jr., Bono, Hugh Grant
- 1961: Eddie Murphy, Woody Harrelson, Barack Obama,
- 1962 Tom Cruise, Demi Moore, Garth Brooks,
- 1963: Brad Pitt, Vanessa Williams, Michael Jordan,

THE COST-OF-LIVING 1963

LIVING:		FOOD:	
New House	$ 12,650	Sugar	90 ₵10 pounds
Avg. Income	$ 5,807	Milk	$1.04/ gallon
New Car	$ 3,233	Coffee	85 ₵/ lb.
Average Rent	$ 110/m	Bacon	69 ₵/ lb.
Movie Ticket	$1.25	Eggs	32 ₵/ dozen
Gasoline	29 ₵ /gal.	Hamburger	40 ₵/ lb.
Stamp	5 ₵	Bread	22 ₵

Part V: Off to College

CHAPTER NINETEEN

FDU

Sometime around November of 1962, while still in high school, I started applying to colleges. There was never any question or doubt that I would be attending college. Not even a discussion. It was simply common knowledge in our family that we would all be attending college.

Among my many choices, I decided to enroll at Fairleigh Dickinson University (FDU) at the Teaneck campus. I did this for a number of reasons. One advantage was that it was only an hour's drive from our home, which meant I could save money by commuting from home, not having to pay for room and board on campus. The other two campuses had a longer commute. Another reason was its reputation for having an outstanding engineering school. And a third had to do with my brother Binnie.

My brother Binnie graduated from high school two years before me and he decided to go to Queens College in Queens, NY. Binnie did extremely well, academically, in high school, scoring in the high 700s on his SATs, but that was high school. Binnie was not able to adjust to college and received low grades in all his subjects except for Science and Math and eventually had to drop out.

My dad was upset with Binnie. So much talent wasted. But he would not give up on Binnie. When I was applying for college, my dad encouraged Binnie to reapply, and one of those schools was FDU. This helped me to decide to go there as well.

Binnie was lucky. It is very difficult to get admitted to another college after being dismissed previously from another school. My path from high school to college was also not easy. Realizing that I had the capacity to do well in school did not help me become a better student. I was still emotionally immature and way too lazy to apply any innate skills that I might have had.

Looking back, I wish I could do it all over again. Being the youngest in my high school classes was tough enough, but when I arrived at college, it was even more challenging. One of the hardships I faced as a freshman in college was that most of the girls were interested in "men." They had no interest in a 17-year-old baby. That, and having the nicknames of 'Brillo', and 'Dumbo', did not help. Nicknames can be brutal, and they did nothing for my self-esteem. I was okay with "Brillo" because my hair was not coarse; it was just curly and wavy. But "Dumbo" hurt.

Growing up with ears that stick out was not easy. My head looked like a taxicab with the doors left open. I remember lying down in bed at night and purposely pressing my ears on the pillow to flatten them out. Thirty minutes on the left ear, then thirty minutes on the right ear. Yes, I really did this, and I did this night after night for about two years. It must have helped because by the time I graduated from college, my ears no longer stuck out. YAY!

CHAPTER TWENTY

Instant Campus Heroes

I will never forget our first day on campus. Both Binnie and I were engineering majors, and we had most of our classes together. We went to school on that first day dressed very casually as we had when we were in high school. It didn't take long for us to see that something was different. As we walked to our first class, we noticed that the male students were all wearing slacks, a dress shirt, and a tie, while the female students were all in pretty dresses. No jeans, no shorts on this warm fall day. Hmm?

As we were about to enter our first class, the professor approached us and said, "Don't you know about the dress code?" Hmm? Obviously, we didn't. Here we are, walking around campus in our jeans, and we are the only ones to do so out of thousands of students.

As we drove home, we kind of chuckled to each other, and then I said to Binnie, "Are you thinking what I'm thinking?" He answered, "You don't like the dress code?" Me: "Nope, not one bit. This is not a Catholic school. Dad is paying a lot of money for us to be here. We should be able to wear whatever we want." Binnie said, "Yep, I agree."

So, we decided to go to school the next day, again, in our normal casual clothes. To our surprise, as we walked to our classes, unlike the day before, we saw quite a few other students, male and female, now wearing jeans. On the third day, about half of all the students throughout the campus were wearing jeans and shorts, and on the fourth day, at least 90% of all the students on campus were dressed casually. WOW. Did we do that?

On Friday, one of our professors approached and informed us that the college Dean wanted to speak to us after our classes. *Oh, Oh! We're in trouble now.?* After our last class, we went to Dean's office, which had a fancy leather desk and mahogany bookshelves. He was dressed in a suit and tie and had a stern look on his face. He looked mean but he was very cordial and nice. Here's how the conversation went.

Dean: I understand what you are doing and why you are doing it. However, we do have rules.
Binnie: "Sir, with all due respect, your rules are archaic and are an infringement on our rights as students who are paying your salary. We did not intend to start a movement; we were simply expressing our right to wear our own choice of clothes.
Dean: "Again, I understand. And I agree with you. However, I still have to answer to the Board of Directors. What do you suggest?" Binnie and I looked at each other.
Me: "How about a compromise?"
Dean: "I'm listening."
Binnie: "How about we wear casual clothes from Monday through Thursday, and we honor your tradition by dressing up on Friday?"
Dean: (Knowing he was fighting a losing cause,) "I can live with that. Let me talk to the Board."

Binnie and I never heard another word about it. As promised, we passed the word about dressing up on Fridays, but within months, almost every student began to continue our casual dress even on Fridays.

So, there you have it. My brother and I challenged a 100-year-old tradition, and we won. In the second week of school, as we were walking around campus, students passed by us with smiles on their faces, and many of them went out of their way to come up to us, slap us on the shoulder, and say, "Way to go". I suppose that's one way to gain popularity, not that we tried.

CHAPTER TWENTY-ONE

So...What's Going On?

- **A Historical Year:**

The year my brother and I both started college, 1963, was a historically memorable one. It was also a notable year for women; Russia became the first country to put a woman in orbit. Congress passed a law to guarantee women equal pay for equal work, and feminist Betty Friedan published The *Feminine Mystique*. I find it strange that it is now 2025 and women are still fighting for equal pay for equal work. *What is taking so long?*

In August of 1963, the charismatic Dr. Martin Luther King, leader of the Civil Rights movement, led the *March on Washington*. It was during his address to the 250,000 people who attended that he gave his famous, *I Have a Dream,* speech. The eyes of the nation were watching, and Americans could sense that a drastic change in race relations in our country was about to happen.

- **November 22nd, 1963: A Fateful Day:**

Just a few months into the school year, President Kennedy was assassinated. My brother and I were both sitting in our 1:00 PM history class when we heard a student standing outside our room begin to shout, "President Kennedy has been shot." Our instructor quickly dismissed the class. My brother and I immediately left class and rushed to our car in the parking lot. We drove the one-hour trip to our parents' home in Dobbs Ferry, New York, and during the drive, as we were listening to the radio, we heard newscaster Walter Cronkite announce that our beloved president had died.

When we arrived home, we found our mom sitting on the couch, crying uncontrollably as she was watching the TV news. As a Catholic, my mom took great pride in our president. She had nothing but love and admiration for this exceptional leader. You did not have to be a Catholic to admire this man. His tragic death was a painful loss to everyone, not just in the United States but throughout the world. No one will ever forget where they were when they heard the terrible news.

Two days later, accused assassin Lee Harvey Oswald was shot and killed by Jack Ruby, a Dallas Nightclub owner. Bizarrely, national TV cameras filmed the entire incident live as it unfolded, and it was witnessed by millions of Americans who were already glued to their TV sets. Vice President Johnson immediately took a jet plane to Washington, D.C., and he was quickly sworn in as the new President of the United States.

A few months later, President Lyndon Johnson, honoring the legacy of President Kennedy, signed the 1964 Civil Rights Act into law. This legislation "outlawed discrimination based on race, color, religion, sex, or national origin." Standing right next to Johnson while he signed the legislation was Dr. Martin Luther King. Very few Americans ever expected a Southern politician to endorse this legislation. Our country was slowly changing.

In August of 1964, the U.S. escalated its involvement in the ongoing Vietnam War. This was a very unpopular war. The American youth vehemently protested this war, and I remember student boycotts and demonstrations on our college campus as well as campuses across the country. Lyndon Johnson was president at the time of our initial involvement and was the recipient of the brunt of these protests, which ultimately led to his decision not to seek a second term for the presidency. By the time our involvement was over, 58,000 young American soldiers had given their lives for their country. The war ended eleven years later in 1975.

Those who were not born in this era have little or no concept of how bad race relations were in the United States at this time in our history. As a small example, there were members of the U.S. Senate filibustered for 47 days in an attempt to block the Civil Rights bill from passing.

Evidently, some politicians were more concerned about their constituents than about doing the right thing. This was a difficult time for our country, but as we always seem to do, we moved ahead, changing ever so slowly.

- **It's Getting Dark:**

So, who remembers **the blackout** that happened on Nov. 9, 1965? All of New York State and the surrounding states on the East Coast went into a total blackout which lasted from 8:00 PM until 7:00 AM. I read somewhere that there was an unusual increase in the birth rate nine months after this event.

- **Music: "The Beatles Are Coming! The Beatles Are Coming"**

In 1963, the British rock group The Beatles had their first American hit, "I Want to Hold Your Hand." In February 1964, the Beatles 'invaded' America. The hype for their arrival on the radio was insane. Instead of "The British are coming, the British are coming," the radio announcers were saying, "The Beatles are coming, the Beatles are coming." The Beatles' trademark, of course, was their incredible music, but they also had another unique trademark: their bowl cut hair. It was a very unique and different hairstyle, and most Americans were not used to it. Below is a photo of the Beatle's first appearance on the Ed Sullivan show.

It appeared to me that the young girls didn't care what kind of hair the Beatles had, or maybe it was their hair that helped perpetuate their mystique. On February 9th, it seemed like every American, and the rest of the world, was glued to their TV sets the night the Beatles appeared on the Ed Sullivan variety TV show. I remember that this was very similar in terms of curiosity to the first appearance of Elvis on the same show years earlier.

That night, on a whim, both my brother and I cut our hair in the style of the Beatles and went to our college classes the next day looking like the first American members of the Beatles' U.S. fan club. This hairstyle worked much better for my brother because he had straight black hair. Not so for me with my curly and bushy brown hair (and my ears sticking out). HA!

The Beatles were just the beginning of British singing groups who became an influential part of the American music landscape. Take a look below at the hits of the '60s.

- "To Sir with Love" - Lulu
- "I'm a Believer" - The Monkees
- "Light My Fire" - The Doors
- "Happy Together" - The Turtles

- "All You Need Is Love" - The Beatles
- "Ruby Tuesday" - The Rolling Stones

The Beatles stole the hearts of American teenagers, but other rock artists and their songs continued to put their stamp on the American culture. There were some great hit songs in 1963, and quite a few of them by female or female groups. Take a look:

- "It's My Party" - Lesley Gore
- "He's So Fine" – The Chiffons
- "Be My Baby" – The Ronettes
- "Heat Wave" – Martha and the Vandellas
- "My Boyfriends Back" – The Angels
- "I Will Follow Him" – Peggy March

I have always felt that music often reflected the changes in society. The age of Rock 'n' Roll of the late '50s and early '60s was slowly becoming a memory. The above list of songs reflects a movement to a softer more meaningful type of music in terms of lyrics and musicality.

It is no surprise that the "Hippie" movement, with its roots in San Franscisco is now spreading nationwide, not only in music, and lifestyle but also in the way we dress. Bell-bottom pants and flowers in ladies' hair are becoming the norm, not the exception. And, yes, I wore those bell-bottomed jeans and wide-collared shirts, just like John Travolta. Oh, did I tell you that I am the one who taught him how to dance? Just kidding.

American artists also had some banner years, such as,

- "Oh Carol" - Neil Sedaka
- "Respect" – Aretha Franklin
- "Sweet Caroline" - Neil Diamond
- "California Dreamin' " - Mama's and the Papas
- "Unchained Melody" - The Righteous Brothers
- "I Can't Help Falling In Love" - Elvis
- "Stand by Me" - Ben E. King

KEN RAND

- "Sound of Silence" - Simon and Garfunkel
- "Under the Boardwalk" - The Drifters
- "Pretty Woman" – Roy Orbinson
- "You Can't Hurry Love" – The Supremes

That's quite a list of great songs and artists and I hope that I didn't leave out your favorites. But you must admit that these songs are distinctly different from the Rock 'n' Roll of "Good Golly, Miss Molly", "Great Balls of Fire" and "Johnny Be Good." Still, the above lists are a handful of great memories.

College parties would often have these songs playing throughout the evening, however, when a party reached the 'later' hours, the songs would slow down, and someone would inevitably play the romantic music of Barbara Steisand *(People)* and Johhny Mathis (*The Twelfth of Never*).

These two artists were, without a doubt, the finest pure vocalists of this era. I know I have mentioned a number of times that my readers should go to YouTube to watch a video, but these two artists are worth it.

- **Television**

I didn't watch too much television while in college but probably more than I should have. There was always something else to do. As did music, television programming went through its own subtle changes. In the 1950's, TV couples were rarely shown in the same bed together. However, in the mid to late '60s, this was a lot more common.

Foul or 'dirty' language was never heard on television and to this day it is still not allowed on mainstream TV. Instead of using the F-word, writers would have the actors say 'freakin'. The words for the male and female organs were not allowed until around 1996. The comedian George Carlin has a famous sketch when he talks about the 'forbidden' words that are not are not allowed on television.

Some of the most popular shows at this time were *The Beverly Hillbillies* (ranked #1), *Bonanza, Candid Camera,* and the game show,

I've Got a Secret. A traditional family sitcom, *The Adventures of Ozzie and Harriet* (the Nelson family) was still going strong and the very handsome and talented Ricky Nelson, their youngest son, became a teenage idol with hit song after hit song.

Sunday night was still family night for TV, which featured the long-lasting Ed Sullivan show. But there was another Sunday night show that captured the entire intrigue of the American audience, and that was *The Fugitive.* In this mystery drama, Dr. Richard Kimble (played by actor David Janssen) was wrongly accused of murdering his wife, and for four years, he became a fugitive of the law. He was finally declared innocent after the capture of the infamous and elusive one-armed man, who was the real murderer. I remember that my mom had a big crush on the handsome actor, David Janssen, and she never missed the opportunity to watch the show.

- **Movies**

Movie censorship was also slowly changing. In 1958 actress Brigitte Bardot sent a culture shock around the world by appearing nude in scenes from the movie, *And God Created Woman.* I was twelve years old when this film debuted. It wasn't until 1968 that the Motion Picture Industry developed its rating system (G, PG, PG-13, R, and X).

Some memorable and classic movies (without nudity) were:

- *The Great Escape* – starring Steve McQueen
- *The Pink Panther* – starring Comedian Peter Sellers (so, so funny)
- *Tom Jones* – won the Oscar for best movie
- *Cleopatra* – starring Elizabeth Taylor and Richard Burton
- *Hud* – starring Paul Newman
- *Lilies of the Field* – starring Sidney Poitier (The first black actor to ever win an Oscar).
- *The Birds* – directed by Alfred Hitchcock

Walking home by myself (about two miles), after watching Alfred Hitchcock's *The Birds,* was an uncomfortable adventure. I left the movie theater around 10:30 at night, and I had a two-mile walk home in the dark (alone). I think I ducked my head down every time I saw a bird. This only lasted for about three weeks. My curly and bushy hair made for a perfect target and nest.

This next story is somewhat embarrassing, but it needs to be told.

CHAPTER TWENTY-TWO

Dr. Davis (aka Economics 101)

- **Lazy Me (aka 'an unexpected outcome')**

I have a great story that perfectly illustrates how poorly I performed as a student when I was in college. No, I am not bragging; I am more than embarrassed about how lazy I was as a student. Again, I wish I could go back to school and start all over. I hope that the end of this story shows more about my character as a person than my lack of effort as a student.

As a freshman, along with every other new FDU entry, I was forced to take Economics 101 with Dr. Davis. Dr. Davis was the only instructor for this course. He was also the only black professor on campus (remember this is 1963). He had a well-deserved reputation for being one of the most demanding professors on campus, and not many students survived his course. He was, in fact, a great instructor; it's just that he was so intimidating.

Dr. Davis was in his early 50s with thin, balding hair, and had a light brown complexion. His most distinguishing feature, other than his mustache, was that he always wore his reading glasses on the tip of his nose.

He was also somewhat old-fashioned. Dr. Davis wore the same light brown suit and blue tie every day and would often boast about his old beat-up 1949 Chevrolet, which he drove to work every day. He would also frequently complain about the "extravagance" of purchasing needless items as a total waste of money. I clearly remember him saying on several occasions, "Why, in the world does anyone need five pairs of shoes?" Evidently, he is not married nor does he know my mom.

Dr. Davis never knew any of his students by name. He didn't care. If he wanted to ask a student a question, which he often did, he would look at his seating chart and call out your name. Are you ready for this?

Dr. Davis: (looking at his seating chart): "Hmm? Mr. Rand, are you here?"

Me: I raised my hand, "I'm here, Dr. Davis."

Dr. Davis: "Mr. Rand, could you explain to me, and the rest of the class, the economic concept of supply and demand?"

Me: *Oh shit...I'm stuck, I didn't do my homework.* "I apologize, Dr. Davis. I didn't have time to do my homework last night."

This was my first mistake.

Dr. Davis: "And why's that, Mr. Rand?"

Me: "I'm on the basketball team, and we didn't get out of practice until about 7:00 PM last night. Then I had to go to Sears & Roebuck and work until 11:00 PM."

Dr. Davis (who is now walking towards me): "Mr. Rand, did you come to this college to play basketball or to get an education?"

Me: "Both." This was my second mistake.

Dr. Davis: "Hmm? Mr. Rand, if you had to choose between playing basketball and receiving an education, then which would you choose?"

Me: (hesitating, and this was my third mistake)

Dr. Davis: "Don't answer that, Mr. Rand. I have an answer for you." With that, he took out a dime and gave it to me.

Me: What's this for?"

Dr. Davis: "I want you to call your mom and tell her to come pick you up from school and take you home. Tell her that I said that you were a worthless student and did not deserve to be here."

Dr. Davis (now inches from my face): "Tell her that you are a waste of space and it is unfair for her son to take the place of another student who would come here to learn."

Me: (almost crying).

I was sitting straight when this inquiry began, and now, I am almost horizontal as if I am ready to be buried underground. Dr. Davis then started to walk back to his desk, and after a few steps turned around, and got right into my face again, and was visibly angry.

Dr. Davis: "I am not finished with you yet, Mr. Rand."

And for the next fifteen minutes, he continued to destroy me and my character. WOW, WOW, WOW! There are no words to explain the sheer humiliation that I was feeling at this moment.

You would think that I learned my lesson from this exchange, but nope, not me. I was just too immature (17 years old) and lazy. I promptly went on to fail the midterm exam. This lack of effort put me in a rather tenuous position. Dr. Davis only gave two exams, a midterm and a final. Do the math. This meant that to get a grade of "C" in the class, I would have to ace the final exam. This is something that I was not likely to do.

About three weeks before the final exam, Dr. Davis made the following announcement to the class. He was standing in front of the room with his glasses at the edge of his nose. Though his glasses looked like they were about to fall off, his eyes were not looking through them; they were looking above the rims, staring at us.

"It seems that quite a few of you lazy freshmen have failed my mid-term exam. Because of this, I am going to give you one more chance to pass this class."

You could hear the knees shaking in the class.

Dr. Davis continued: "Your only chance to pass this class is to come to my S.U." A very brave student asked: "What's an S.U. Dr. Davis?"

Dr. Davis: "The S.U. is my personal **S**ize **U**p of you. You are invited to come to my office on the morning of June 2nd, where I will give you a one-on-one oral final exam."

Not sure if you have ever taken an oral school exam for a course, but it is much more difficult than a 'paper' test, and you can't B.S. your way out of it. No choice. I had to go.

Dr. Davis's office was on the fourth floor of an old Victorian home. This beautiful old building had a winding staircase (and of course, no elevator). When I arrived at this majestic-looking building, there was a line of over 50 students waiting for their turn to take the oral exam. That line of students stretched from the lobby on the first floor all the way up the stairs to the fourth floor where he had his office.

There were so many of us that Dr. Davis decided to take 5 – 7 of us at a time. It was frightening and intimidating. Students were walking back down the stairs after taking their oral exam, and they were either physically shaking or in tears. We asked them about the exam, but they were too shaken up to talk. Some of them looked like they were about to throw up.

This did not look good. It was kind of like waiting outside a dentist's office and hearing patients scream in pain before it was your turn to go in and thanks to Dr. Rosen, our family dentist, I was only too familiar with these cries of agony.

After about two hours of waiting on the staircase, there were only seven of us left to be interviewed. We were now at the top of the winding staircase directly outside his door, waiting to be slaughtered.

Dr. Davis came out of his office, looked us over, and told all seven of us to come in (and he wasn't smiling). So, here's the scene. The seven of us are in a huge attic-type room with a vaulted ceiling. Dr. Davis is sitting at his leather-covered desk that appears to be a hundred years old, and we are lined up about 10 feet away. It looked and felt like the infamous Saturday night massacre from the Al Capone story.

Dr. Davis: "I'm tired, so I have only one question for all of you. Each of you will take a turn answering the question and be prepared to back up your answer with sound economic reasoning. Here is your question. There seems to be a surplus of food in the United States, and my simple question to you is, what would you do with it? Remember to back up your answer with sound economic reasoning."

One student, after another, tried to sound ultra-smart, discussing the theory of supply and demand, and whether they would either destroy the food or store it for a later day. It finally became my turn to offer my words of wisdom.

Me: "Dr. Davis, I would give the food away."
Dr. Davis (with a quizzical look): "Hmm? You look very familiar. What's your name, son?" *Oh ____, he remembers me. I'm dead. It's over.*
Me (visibly shaking and in my lowest voice): "Myy nammme is Ken Rand."
Dr. Davis: "I knew you looked familiar. This should be fun. Tell me, Mr. Rand, why would you give the food away?"
Me (still shaking): "Dr. Davis, there are people in the United States who are homeless and hungry. It doesn't make sense to destroy or store the food."
Dr. Davis: "Hmm? Interesting, but can you back it up with sound economic reasoning?"
Me: I thought for a minute and then said, "No, I'm sorry, Dr. Davis. It just seems like the right thing to do."

Dr. Davis looked around at the other students, and asked them, "Would any of you like to argue with Mr. Rand and punch holes in his answer?" One by one, each student reaffirmed their answers and repeated their argument that giving away food for free would not be a sound economic solution.

Dr. Davis: "Mr. Rand. I am going to give you one more chance. Either change your answer or back it up with economic reasoning."
Me: "Dr. Davis, I will not change my answer."
Dr. Davis: "Why, and don't give me crap about people being hungry."

I thought for almost a full minute and finally said: "Dr. Davis, if you feed hungry people, then they will be healthier. If people are healthy, then they can go to work. If they go to work, they can earn a living. If they make money, then they can spend money. If they spend money, they are helping the economy."

Dr. Davis: "You are all dismissed."

I walked out of that room shaking like a leaf. Usually, walking down a staircase is easier than walking up, but not this time. All I could do now was wait for my grade, which I was sure would be an "F."

A week later, I received all my grades in the mail. I couldn't wait to see my grades for economics. I was totally shocked when I received a "B" for the year. End of story.

CHAPTER TWENTY-THREE

More Great College Stories

- **So Many Pancakes!**

This story has an incredible ending.

When my brother and I went to FDU, our dad made a deal with us. He would help by buying us a new car, making half the payments. The condition was that we stayed away from college fraternities for two years. We, of course, agreed.

At the beginning of my third year (1965), one of the fraternities approached me with an offer I could not refuse. They wanted me to play on their basketball intramural team. They went on to tell me that they would exempt me from any hazing, and they would cover my daily lunch expenses for as long as I was on the team. Sounded good to me.

That year, we won the intramural championship. A few months later, the International House of Pancakes franchise hosted a college promotion featuring a joint fraternity and sorority pancake-eating contest. Not only was I good at basketball, but I was also good at eating. I was the type who would scavenge from my classmates' leftovers when we had lunch. It seemed like I had a bottomless pit for a stomach, and I became an easy choice to represent our fraternity. I did not know my sorority partner and we met for the first time on the day of the contest. All I can say is that she was wider than me.

A few weeks before the contest, I received a list of the rules in the mail. *Rules? Who needs rules?* I thought that all I had to do was eat as much as I could. The rules went on to say that we had half an hour to eat as many pancakes as possible. There was a list of other meaningless rules, and I almost stopped reading until the last rule caught my eye. This rule said that any food that was still in your mouth at the end of the time limit would count towards your total. *Hmmm? I instantly had a plan.*

Oh, I almost forgot to mention. Along with the rules, there were some suggestions. One of them was not to diet before the contest. Dieting would shrink your stomach, preventing you from eating more. Another one that surprised me was that we should avoid drinking anything (even water) while eating during the contest. Again, this would probably fill our stomachs and limit our food intake.

The day has finally arrived. The International House of Pancakes was only a short walk from campus. It was packed. There were over 200 FDU students there, including all of my frat brothers, along with the sorority sisters of my partner. I think there were about 20 teams, all of us sitting at a long table. My partner was directly opposite me.

Good news. The pancakes were not the standard size. They were only about 2" wide. Cool. We were informed in advance that each plate we ordered would contain 18 pancakes.

Okay. Let's get ready to rumble.

Within the first fifteen minutes, I finished five plates. That's a total of 90 pancakes. My partner? I never looked at her. I was too focused on myself. My frat brothers were going crazy. I heard a few of them shout, "You're in the lead. Go..Go..Go."

Oh boy. It's now getting difficult to swallow. My mouth was incredibly dry, and I was dying for a glass of water, but I remembered the suggestion to avoid drinking water. The pancakes were beginning to taste like chalk (not that I ever ate a piece of chalk).

I had to slow down. I took off from eating for about 10 minutes, and my frat brothers went silent. I tried to eat a few more pancakes, but I just couldn't put another pancake in my mouth. I could feel the disappointment of my brothers. But remember, I had a plan.

Before I could initiate my plan, I started to hear noises from the teams along the table. These were not pleasant noises. Apparently, one by one, some teams were dropping out for obvious reasons. I did not dare to look up because it was painfully obvious what was happening. I was later told that it was very gross. I kept telling myself, "Focus. Focus."

There are now five minutes to go, and my frat brothers are screaming at me. "Come on, Ken. You can do it. Keep going." I finally ordered another plate, and my frat brothers went wild. I began to think about my plan, but it was too soon to initiate it. There is now a minute to go, and I could hear my brothers screaming and yelling, "EAT…EAT…EAT." But it was too soon.

Thirty seconds to go. Fifteen seconds to go. **Here it comes**.

I began to roll up all the pancakes on my plate into a ball. *"What's he doing?"* 5…4…3…I took the ball of 18 pancakes and shoved it into my mouth. I could hear….2…1…Then, without any warning, my partner threw up, and most of it went all over me. OMG. How gross, but … it's over. I think there is a famous scene in the movie "Sandlot" when the young boys have a similar experience.

As I planned, those 18 pancakes contributed towards my score, bringing my total 108 pancakes. My embarrassed partner ate 138 pancakes, most of which were all over me. We came in 3rd place. Not bad. The winning couple ate a total of 257 pancakes, with the guy consuming 198 (he was a college football player) and his partner, a cheerleader, eating only 59. The prize for first place was a two-week trip to Hawaii. The prize for 3rd place was free pancakes for the rest of the year at the International House of Pancakes. Not that I ever wanted to see or eat another pancake for the rest of my life.

This story is not over yet:

As luck would have it, a few weeks later, I was invited by my high school girlfriend to take her to the Senior Prom. Of course, we had a great time. That was until the morning after. About eight of us stayed overnight at her friend's house, and we made plans to visit Jones Beach the next day.

I woke up the next morning to the smell of bacon and went down to the kitchen only to see my plate full of three large pancakes.

Oh no…how can I say "No?". You need to understand that I never wanted to eat another pancake as long as I lived. Some choices are not so easy. I had to be polite.

In this next story, my dancing skills will soon shine again.

- **Dancin' Machine**

This story took place in my junior year at college (1966,) and I thought you might enjoy it.

It was in the month of November when my friends invited Me and my brother Binnie to a local TV dance show on a Friday afternoon. There were about 16 of us who decided to attend. Each week, this show had a dance contest, which we were all aware of. My brother, Binnie, was with his future wife, Linda, and I was with my regular dance partner, Marney.

On the drive down to the TV studio, Binnie leaned over to me and whispered in my ear, "Do you mind if we switch dance partners?" Surprised, I whispered back, "Why?" He was honest and said, "I think I have a better chance of winning the contest with your partner." I thought about it for a minute and asked him, "Does Linda know?" He said, "Not yet." I smiled and wondered how she would take this news. I am competitive, and I also wanted to win, but I was also very confident in both Linda and me, and I told him, "OK, we'll switch. Good luck."

There were at least twenty-four other couples on the dance floor when the contest started. Remember, this was on TV, so it was kind of a big deal. If you were tapped on the shoulder by a judge, it meant that you had to leave the dance floor. One by one, the other couples left the floor, and as fate would have it, it was now down to two couples. Binnie with my original partner, Marney, and me, with Binnie's future wife, Linda.

Guess who won. Ha! To my brother's great disappointment, Linda and I won. Thank you, Linda. You made me look good. The funny thing is that I don't remember what the first prize was. I guess beating my brother was good enough for me (and especially for Linda). Again, winning feels good.

• Time For Some Self-Reflection.

Beating my brother at dance contests, felt great. But it was not good enough to repair my broken self-esteem. College was a difficult time for me, especially when it came to dating. During my first two years of college, I think I broke the Guiness Book of Records, for blind dates.

At the time of this dance contest, Binnie and I were living in an apartment with two college friends. It was an easy commute to school, in that we were only about a mile from campus. This was my first real taste of freedom and as expected, I was too young and immature to appreciate it. Our apartment was constantly visited by friends which made it difficult to focus on school. Not that I needed an excuse, but there was always someone wanting to play cards, watch TV, listen to music and, of course, there were the weekend parties.

Binnie was already dating Linda, and their relationship was serious. I had little doubt that they would eventually marry. I was now dating Ellen O'Brien and I was in constant fear that this free-loving flower child would dump me as soon as she was intrigued by someone else. I met Ellen while working in our family-owned ice cream store.

This insecurity brought back some past experiences where I was always comparing myself to my brother. Binnie, who had an IQ of 161,was also very confident and very good-looking. Everything seemed to come so easy for him. Girlfriends, grades, friends, etc. Comparing myself to him was a losing battle. This was unfair for me to do to myself. But I did it, nevertheless.

Reflecting back, at this time, I was in a constant mode of self-pity. Those old high school feelings of worthlessness were returning. Things got worse in our senior year, when Binnie and I moved to another apartment and lived by ourselves. This is not really true. We did not live alone. Binnie's girlfriend, Linda, was with us practically every day. When I came home from school, the two of them were always lovey-dovey, and this just added fuel to the fire. My self-pity was reaching new heights. I simply did not have the emotional tools to deal with it.

When Ellen broke up with me a month after graduation and started dating someone else, I once again went into a deep depression constantly reinforcing my belief that I was "not good enough", and "that something must be wrong with me". Looking back, my self-pity was a colossal waste of time and effort. The only thing wrong with me was my false narrative that something was wrong with me. As I earlier wrote, it wasn't until I was 40 years old and I went to the Forum Conference in San Jose, CA., when my life changed, and I chose to no longer feel sorry for myself. Get over it. It's time to move on.

- **The Ice Cream Store (1965 – 67)**

It may be the dream of every kid to own and work in an Ice Cream store, but it definitely wasn't mine. In 1965, my parents bought and opened a Carvel Ice Cream store. Carvel stores are located throughout the East Coast, and they were the first ice cream franchise, even before Dairy Queen and Baskin-Robbins. They were known for their great-tasting and freshly made soft ice cream, cakes, and variety of flavors. The reason my parents bought the store was to offer steady employment to my brother, Frankie, as its full-time manager. Our store was in a town called New City, which had a population of about 25,000 people. New City was the center of Rockland County, located about 10 miles west of the Tappan Zee Bridge, which separated Rockland from Westchester.

The pretty young lady in front of the store (Linda Reger) was a waitress and the daughter of the owner of the Crossroads restaurant next door. Not only was she our neighbor, but Frankie soon fell in love with Linda, and they were married a few years later in 1968.

I had a love/hate relationship with our store. Frankie worked there from Monday through Friday, but my brother, Binnie, and I, while attending college, had to work there on weekends. The days and nights we had to work at the store became an intrusion on our free time. Yes, I did earn a moderate salary, but I would rather have been doing anything else. Attending college classes every day and then working weekends was not in my plans.

Unlike other ice cream franchises, we had to make our own ice cream at the store. It was impossible to do this during the week, so we would often make over 30 different flavors on Friday evenings, which would take us into the early hours of the morning.

I love to eat ice cream but making it until 3:00 AM was something that took away from the great taste of a chocolate marshmallow Sunday. Here are some interesting stories about my time at the store.

- **Another Peanut Butter Story**

One Saturday, a very attractive young lady walked into the store and asked me if we had peanut butter and jelly ice cream. *What?*

Peanut Butter ice cream? I told her we had over 30 flavors of ice cream, but none of them had peanut butter. She was really cute. *Hmmm, what to do?*

I told her that I also love peanut butter and jelly and that if she came in next weekend, I would have it for her. Well, I made this strange flavor of ice cream. I poured vanilla ice cream into the machine and while it came out of the nozzle, I simply added spoon fills of peanut butter and grape jelly during this process. And yes, she did come to the store the next weekend. The problem was that she was the only person who ever ate it.

Two weeks go by, three weeks go by, and no one else even tastes a sample of it. Here we are, left with a 5-gallon can of peanut butter and jelly ice cream that no one but this very cute girl even asked for it The unused ice cream was taking up space needed in our showcase, so I eventually had to discard it. Anyway…there were many other cute girls who frequented our store.

- **The Pink Sprinkles**

On the East Coast, we had chocolate and multi-colored sprinkles that we would put on top of an ice cream cone or sundae. I believe that in other parts of the country, they are called "jimmies".

Frankie had this gimmick to test new girls who worked in the store. One day I walked into the store, and I saw a newly hired girl separating the sprinkles. Confused, I went to the back of the store and asked Frankie, "What is she doin?". He laughed, then said that he told her that the pink sprinkles were 'defective' and that they needed to be separated. I laughed so hard. I told Frankie that this was cruel and unusual punishment. He told me that he was just bored and wanted to have some fun. Frankie had a good sense of humor.

- **Frozen Solid**

Besides ice cream cones and sundaes, we also created a variety of specialty items, including ice cream cakes and ice cream logs. These ice cream logs were made with a roll of cake and a roll of ice cream, topped with any desired flavor of ice cream.

The logs were a good seller, except during wintertime, when it was generally too cold to eat any ice cream. However, one day in January, a customer came in and told me he wanted an ice cream log for his daughter who asked for one for her birthday party. I vaguely remembered that we had one log left over from the summer and that it might be in the freezer below the counters. Sure enough, I found it. I'm pretty certain that it had remained frozen for over four months, and it was rock-hard. In fact, it was so frozen that he would probably need an electric saw to cut it into slices. However, a sale is a sale.

I told him, "We have one left. Do you want it?" He was ecstatic that he could fulfill his daughter's wish, and he bought it and went home. Meanwhile, I am immediately regretting selling him this frozen solid log. There is no way he'll be able to slice it. No way.

Two weeks later, the same customer returns to the store, and I'm thinking he's going to yell at me and ask for his money back. Instead, he said, "That's the best-tasting ice cream dessert my family has ever had. You made my daughter very happy." And then he handed me a $10 tip. Go figure, huh?

- **Finally, Some College Success**

Though I was not the best college student, I did have some rare moments of success. Despite my lack of effort in college, it's surprising to me that my brain retained much more than I expected. I'm a big fan of the TV game show "Jeopardy," and I'm constantly surprised by my knowledge and ability to recall the right questions to their answers.

There are very few things in college that I am proud of, but one of them is my junior-year English term paper on William Blake. I'm not sure why or how Blake became the subject of my thesis, but the more research I did, the more I became in awe of this man's genius.

He was a poet, artist, and engraver, and he excelled at all three. He is most famous for his *Songs of Innocence* (1789) and *Songs of Experience (1795)* as well as *The Marriage of Heaven and Hell*, (1793).

Below are the opening lines to one of his most famous poems, *Tyger, Tyger.*

> Tyger! Tyger! burning bright
> *A Time Like No Other*
> In the forests of the night,
> What immortal hand or eye
> Could frame thy fearful symmetry?

His poems were considered radical at that time, in that he questioned the foundations of organized religion. His use of symbolism and satire surpassed that of any other poet I have ever read.

Another term paper (this one in my senior year) that I am also proud of was about the writer, poet, environmental scientist, and philosopher, Henry David Thoreau. He is best known for his work titled *Walden, or Life in the Woods (1854)*. In this work, he relates his real-life experiences of living on Walden Pond, a property owned by his philosopher friend, Ralph Waldo Emerson. The fact that I was even able to understand his writing and write about it myself was beyond my expectations for my own intellect. I received a well-earned grade of "A" on both papers.

Graduation is just a month away and I am lost and confused. What do I do now?

CHAPTER TWENTY-FOUR

What Now?

It is May of 1967. I am barely 21 years old, and I will soon be graduating with a Bachelor of Science degree in mathematics. What happened to engineering? Good question. All it took was one semester of college physics, and my engineering career was over. Although I managed to earn a grade of "B" in physics, I didn't think I deserved it. My mid-term test was an embarrassing 53%. My brother Binnie received an "A" in physics, but he earned his "A" with a 97% average.

Even though I passed my Physics course, I began to wonder what kind of bridge I could build with a 53% average. How long would it take before that bridge would surely collapse? Not wanting to be responsible for the deaths of hundreds of people, I quickly switched my major from engineering to mathematics.

As someone who was about to graduate from college, I had one major problem. With just a few months to go, I still had no idea what I wanted to do with my life. Becoming a teacher was not a thought that crossed my mind. I did have a fantasy about being a sports statistician, but I never pursued it for a couple of reasons.

For one, I was very idealistic and wanted to change the world. This would not be easy to do as a sports statistician. Secondly, I also had fantasies of being a professional basketball player (yes, I did), which was way better than being a sports statistician. However, becoming a pro athlete was not meant to be. Though I was good enough to play college basketball, and I was an excellent shooter, my short height of 5'11" and inability to dribble a basketball (stop laughing) put an end to my basketball career. Fantasy over.

Little did I know at that time that my basketball shooting skills would eventually come in handy as a teacher. As college graduation drew near, I remember being extremely envious of my friends who knew where their future lay. I would often think, *It's just not fair.* I was so very confused and lost. I suspect that many people reading this can relate to my feelings.

I was even envious of my brother, who was also graduating with me. With multiple degrees in engineering, he already had an offer from Grumman Aircraft to work on the Apollo Moon project. At least he knew what his immediate future would be.

About a month before graduation, a representative from the Peace Corps (an international program originated by President John F. Kennedy and Pierre Salinger) came to the Fairleigh Dickinson campus. The more I thought about it, the more the Peace Corps seemed like a good fit for me, especially since I didn't have a job waiting for me when I graduated. I also thought that traveling to a foreign country would be a great experience.

With that in mind, I impulsively signed up. The Corps soon had me take some of their tests, and based on the results, assigned me to a teaching post in Kenya. Time was moving relatively quickly, too quickly, and I had only one month after graduation to prepare for my trip to Kenya.

• **Graduation**

On graduation day, the temperature was 93 degrees, and the humidity was 97%. This is as uncomfortable as it can get. Especially when the ceremony took over three hours. And….it was in a tent, which made it even more difficult to bear. But it was a special day, and we endured.

Binnie, whose birth name was James, should have graduated before me because the names were supposed to be announced alphabetically; however, someone made a mistake and listed my name, 'Kenneth', first. So what? Well, this officially made me the first person in our family (other than my dad), to graduate from college. Big deal, huh? Not really. Looking back, I was lucky that my math and science grades were good enough to allow me to graduate.

Of course, our parents attended the ceremony. Binnie invited his college girlfriend, Linda Sachs, and I invited my girlfriend, Ellen who recently enrolled in Boston University. We had the usual graduation party at our parents' home in Dobbs Ferry with my mom's family there to help us celebrate. I remember feeling numb and lost throughout the entire day. I'm thinking, *what do I do now? Do I really want to go to Kenya?*

• **What Will My Future Be?**

I am not sure why I didn't tell my dad right away about my new job with the Peace Corps, but I broke the news to him about two weeks before I was scheduled to leave to Kenya. After the shock wore off, my dad confronted me with 21 questions, the most important of which was "Why?" I idealistically told him that I wanted to change the world.

He then looked at me with his wise and proud eyes, smiled, and said, "You can change the world right here. Why go to Africa?" He went on to say, "Instead of teaching in Africa, you can teach here (in Westchester County, New York) or if not here, then maybe in New York City." At that time, we lived only about 30 miles from the city. I must admit he had a good point, but there was a minor problem: I did not have a teaching license, a detail that the Peace Corps did not care about.

With the help of one of my dad's best friends, Meyer Packer, I was able to enroll in a free master's program at City University of New York. The tradeoff for obtaining a free master's degree and a teaching license was that I had to be willing to sacrifice two years of my professional life, teaching in the New York City public school system.

In 1967, there was a significant shortage of teachers in NYC, and possibly nationwide, particularly in math and science. The city was desperate, and this new program was a result of that desperation.

Veteran teachers even had a name for those of us who enrolled and graduated from this summer program. They called us the "60-day wonders."

Sadly, I found my summer graduate courses in education to be boring. Our graduate school instructors knew that we were on a conveyor belt to obtain a teaching license, so they tried to cram as much knowledge and theory as possible into an eight-week summer session. Staying awake in those classes was quite a challenge. My graduate instructors were a great example of the kind of teacher that I did not want to be.

Within a few weeks, I would soon find out what kind of teacher I was meant to be. My forty-seven incredible years of teaching are chronicled in my book, *One Student at a Time: A Teacher's Journey.*

CHAPTER TWENTY-FIVE

Brown's Hotel: The End of an Era

Brown's Hotel, during my college years, was thriving. My dad was still the band leader, a job he would have until he retired in 1986 at the age of 70. Since I was working at the Carvel ice cream store during college, my time visiting the hotel was limited. However, it was a Thursday in the summer of 1965 when my dad called me and told me that I might want to come to the hotel and spend the weekend. His reason for that request is that it was rumored that Jerry Lewis was almost certainly going to make an appearance at the hotel. I drove up that Friday. I made a good choice.

- **Second Jerry Lewis Story**

    As my dad predicted, Jerry Lewis did show up. Mr Lewis prided himself on being a good athlete (which he was), and when he stayed at the hotel, he would often involve himself in the Saturday afternoon softball game between the hotel staff and the guests.

    As I walked up the hill to the softball field, I heard him shouting, "I need a glove. I need a glove." When he saw me, he noticed my baseball glove and said, "Hey, kid, can I borrow your glove?" I said, "Sure, Mr. Lewis." Of course, the game drew a large crowd and was fun, especially when Jerry Lewis hit a home run.

    After the game, he approached me and said, "Kid, how much do you want for your glove? I really like it." Shocked, I told him,

"Mr. Lewis, this is my favorite glove, I'm not sure I want to sell it." He said, "How about $50?" (The glove only cost me $12). With a polite smile, I said, "No, thank you Mr. Lewis," and I walked away. He followed me and said, "How about $100?" So, I suppose you could say he made me an offer I couldn't refuse. He took out a roll of $100 bills and gave me one, which I put in my pocket. He said, "Thanks, kid." I said, "thank you Mr. Lewis. You are one of my favorite entertainers." He smiled and said, "Thank you kid." I later took that $100 and bought a new glove, a bat, and some baseballs, and still had money left over.

- **A Cultural Change:**

In the late 1970s, vacationing in the Catskills and staying at hotels like Brown's slowly lost their appeal. Air travel was becoming an easy way to go on vacation, opening up new options for families. Places like Atlantic City and Las Vegas became popular destinations and alternative choices.

For those who frequently visited the Catskills in the '50s and '60s, this was a painful experience. It was a way of life that was disappearing. It was a cultural shock to those of us who spent our growing years and our summers in the Catskills.

Brown's Hotel was later destroyed in a fire on April 14, 2012. Another part of my past is gone forever. I am so thankful for the wonderful and exciting experiences that I had during my summers at the hotel. Reflecting back upon those summers, I realized that my fourteen years of experiences at the hotel helped to balance, in a positive way, the roller coaster ride that was my life.

Summer is over, and I now find myself looking back on the totality of my life experiences. Was there drama? Yes, of course. But there were so many more great things that happened to me as compared to the traumatic events I went through. Both the good and bad helped me to become who I am today. Life is a learning process, and I am still learning.

As a teacher, I clearly recall my last day in the classroom, standing in front of my students, thinking that I was a better teacher on that day than I had been the day before. Maybe the rollercoaster ride is not over?

- **In Conclusion:**

I hope I have been able to accomplish two things. One is to bring you down memory lane, and the other is to weave in my fascinating life experiences along the way.

As I said in my Introduction, I am not a fan of living in the past, but I am a big fan of the past. My only hope is that we as a civilization and society are able to learn from our past mistakes.

Even though times have and will continue to change (Are you ready for AI?). There is no doubt in my mind, and among those of us who also lived in the 1950s and 1960s, that this period was a special and a distinct time in American history. For most of us who were brought up in this era, it was truly "A Time Like No Other."

BREAKING NEWS 1964 - 1967!

Did you know that in 1964

- The U.S. population is now 192 million people
- The U.S. Congress passed the Civil Rights Act ending segregation.
- The Beatles make their American debut on the Ed Sullivan show.
- Martin Luther King received the Nobel Peace prize.

1965

- Black leader Malcolm X is assassinated in New York.
- In Los Angeles, the Watts neighborhood experiences riots resulting in major casualties.
- Soviet cosmonaut Alexei Leonov, became the first human to walk in space.

1966

- Miranda rights are established by the U.S. Supreme Court.
- The Soviets spaceship lands on the moon

1967

- The U.S. population is now 199 million. Life expectancy is 71 years.
- San Francisco becomes the epicenter of the "Hippie" movement during the "Summer of Love".
- Isreal wins the Six-Day War in their conflict with Egypt, Jordan, and Syria

Famous People Born:

- **1964:** Michele Obama, Russell Crowe, Simon Cowell, Sandra Bullock, Barry Bonds.
- **1965**: Viola Davis, Ben Stiller, Dr. Dre, Robert Downey Jr., Shania Twain.
- **1966**: Halle Berry, Janet Jackson, Adam Sandler, Patrick Dempsey.
- **1967**: Julia Roberts, Nicole Kidman, Will Ferrell, Jason Statham.

THE COST-OF-LIVING 1967

LIVING:

- New House $ 14,495
- Avg. Income $ 7,300
- New Car $ 2,724
- Average Rent $ 125/m
- Movie Ticket $1.25
- Gasoline   33 ₵ /gal.
- Stamp   5 ₵

FOOD:

- Sugar   60 ₵/10 pounds
- Milk $1.15/ gallon
- Coffee   90 ₵/ lb.
- Bacon   74 ₵/ lb.
- Eggs   38 ₵/ dozen
- Hamburger 48 ₵/ lb.
- Bread   22 ₵

EPILOGUE

It is 1967, and as Bob Dylan poetically wrote, 'The times they are a-Changin'. We are no longer living in a time of innocence.

Five years after the assassination of President Kennedy in 1963, civil rights leader Martin Luther King was also assassinated. Three months later, Kennedy's younger brother, Senator Robert Kennedy, who was the frontrunner for the democratic nomination, was gunned down and killed in Los Angeles moments after he gave a victory speech for winning the California primary. People are asking, "What is wrong with our country"? This sounds all too familiar.

In the summer of 1969. I was in Florence, Italy, and I was fortunate to watch, at a local television store, our Apollo spacecraft land on the moon. American Neil Armstrong became the first human to step on the moon. This was an amazing technological achievement. It was with great pride that I heard American Neil Armstrong's famous quote, "That's one small step for man, one giant leap for mankind".

After my summer vacation in Europe (1969), I went back to the U.S. and visited my dad at the hotel, and as luck would have it, I was able to attend the Woodstock festival, which was nearby. This event brought together over 500,000 music lovers, who for three days were dancing and getting high in the muddy rain. No, I didn't get high, and yes, I got soaking wet.

Thousands enjoying the music.   Having fun in the mud.

Speaking about drugs…there were a few hit records in the late '60s dedicated to the use of drugs. One of them was "White Rabbit" by Jefferson Airplane, another one was "Lucy is the Sky with Diamonds", by the Beatles and then there was "I Want to Take You Higher" by Sly and the Family Stone. I cannot imagine those songs being written or recorded in the '50s. Music is always a sign of the times.

My brother and I love to go out dancing, but it was almost impossible to go to a party or dance club and not be overwhelmed by the odor of marijuana. Though dancing was our 'high', you didn't even have to smoke weed to get high.

In a few years, it will be the early 70s, when so much will change and will continue to change. Newspaper headlines, on a daily basis, are still highlighting the American death toll from the Vietnam War. The Civil Rights movement is growing in strength, but it is meeting with resistance, and there are numerous race riots throughout major cities.

Violence throughout the country is steadily increasing. Soon to come there will be another significant change. Our increasing diversity is extending not only to ethnicity but also to the numerous new opportunities for us to enjoy a variety of forms of communication and entertainment.

In the early 2000s' and on a more impactful level, computers and cell phones are advancing rapidly. Their advantages are obvious, but some of us old folks are finding it to be a difficult adjustment. We have also seen a shift in television programming, where talk shows and 24-hour news channels have become a staple of daily programming, and they are available at any time of the day or night. Game shows are more popular than ever, and in the last twenty years, talent shows such as The Voice, America's Got Talent, and American Idol have offered us a chance to view talent that we were not able to see before.

The rise in the popularity of rap and hip-hop music is also part of this growth and change, and the women's rights movement is gaining momentum. We no longer have to read a book by holding it; we can now 'listen' to it in various ways. Podcasts and blogging are also new forms of sharing and communicating. Given a choice, I would rather read a book by holding it in my hands.

We have also seen a shift in television programming, where talk shows and 24-hour news channels have become a staple of daily programming, and they are available at any time of the day or night. Game shows are more popular than ever, and in the last twenty years, talent shows such as The Voice, America's Got Talent, and American Idol have offered us a chance to view talent that we were not able to see before. The rise in the popularity of rap and hip-hop music is also part of this growth and change, and the women's rights movement is gaining momentum.

One of my favorite things to do when I'm bored (which is rare) is to watch the incredible talent that is available on Instagram, featuring comedians, musicians, singers, and dancers. Another significant change is that today's athletes are bigger, stronger, faster, and better than at any time in sports history. That's not to say that there weren't great athletes when I was growing up.

- **More About Me:**

This book ends in the year 1967. After I graduated college at the age of 21, I soon became a math teacher in a Junior High School in the Southeast Bronx. The problem is that I do not know how to teach. It took a few years but with my passion for teaching, I made it a lifelong goal to be the best at what I do. My next forty-seven years is a roller coaster ride both in life and in teaching and it is chronicled in my memoir, "One Student at a Time: A Teacher's Journey."